THE BHS COMPLETE TRAINING MANUAL FOR

STAGE 3

The
British
Horse
Society

THE BHS COMPLETE TRAINING MANUAL FOR

STAGE 3

Islay Auty FBHS

Updated and revised by
Margaret Linington-Payne MA (Ed) BHSI

KENILWORTH PRESS

First published in the UK in 2005 as The BHS Training Manual for Stage 3
by Kenilworth Press, an imprint of Quiller Publishing Ltd
This revised and updated edition with the new title The BHS Complete Training Manual for Stage 3 published 2011

British Library Cataloguing-in-Publication Data
   A catalogue record for this book
   is available from the British Library

ISBN 978 1 905693 27 6

Line drawings by Dianne Breeze and Carole Vincer
Line diagrams by Michael J Stevens

Book and cover design by Sharyn Troughton
Printed in Malta by Gutenberg Press Ltd.

Kenilworth Press

An imprint of Quiller Publishing
Wykey House, Wykey, Shrewsbury, SY4 1JA
Tel: 01939 261616 Fax: 01939 261606
E-mail: info@quillerbooks.com
Website: www.kenilworthpress.co.uk

Contents

Picture Acknowledgements

All line drawings are by Dianne Breeze, with the exception of those on pages 60, 61, 62, 74, 75 and 76, which are by Carole Vincer.

The jumping diagrams are by Michael J. Stevens

Picture sources
The author and publishers wish to acknowledge the following books as sources for some of the illustrations:

- *The BHS Complete Manual of Equitation*, Consultant Editor Patrick Print OBE FBHS, published by Kenilworth Press

- *The BHS Complete Manual of Stable Management Second Edition*, Revised and updated by Josephine Batty-Smith BHSI, published by Kenilworth Press

- *No Foot, No Horse*, by Gail Williams and Martin Deacon, published by Kenilworth Press

- *Threshold Picture Guide No. 16, Feet and Shoes*, by Toni Webber, published by Kenilworth Press

- *Threshold Picture Guide No. 43, Functional Anatomy*, by Dr Chris Colles BVetMed, PhD, MRCVS, published by Kenilworth Press

How to Use This Book

The aim of this book is to provide students working towards Stage 3 with detailed guidance to help prepare thoroughly for the examination. The information is laid out as follows:

The individual elements of each subject that you will be assessed on are listed under a broad category heading, e.g. Clothing, Saddlery, etc.

Each topic has a section on **'What the assessor is looking for'**, which breaks down the subject matter required, giving a fuller picture of the level of information required or what you might be asked to do.

The sections entitled **'How to become competent'** give you the knowledge and practical skills required to be successful.

Throughout, the book is aiming to clearly outline the requirements of the syllabus, and give you a sound basis of the knowledge required.

The information is set out in two sections: Horse Knowledge and Care, and Riding. The Horse Knowledge and Care is divided into 5 units. Each unit of the exam can be taken separately on different occasions, or they can be tackled together on the same examination day. If you pass the Horse Knowledge and Care section you will be given the EQL Level 3 Diploma in BHS Horse Knowledge and Care, which indicates that you are competent to care for up to four horses/ponies with minimal supervision. The attainment of the Riding section (EQL Level 3 Diploma in BHS Riding Horses), together with the Horse Knowledge and Care section, gives you the full Stage 3 certificate.

There are no short cuts to achieving practical competence. 'Practice makes perfect' may be an old saying but it still holds good today. Your past experience with horses, which should already be providing you with a sound foundation of practical competence, will be tested more searchingly at this level. And your practical ability to 'read' horses and be aware of how best to handle or ride them will be challenged a little more pointedly. The book should enable you to build both ability and confidence, giving you a very clear, structured reference to your progress towards attempting and achieving the required standard.

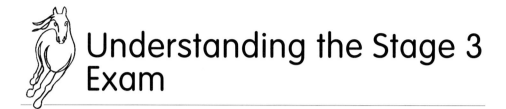

Understanding the Stage 3 Exam

After Stage 2

After your success in passing Stage 2 the sensible route is confidently to consolidate your knowledge before you start to think about Stage 3. Unless you have come to BHS exams a little later in life and therefore have a wealth of practical hands-on experience with horses, which can help you to 'fast track' the exams, do not aim for Stage 3 too soon after passing Stage 2. Just as after taking GCSE exams it takes another training commitment to aim for 'A' levels, so it is with Stage 2 and Stage 3. No two people are the same, and it is therefore pointless to give an optimum length of study time between Stages 2 and 3. Suffice it to say that at Stage 3 the standard of both the riding and the stable management are considerably more challenging than at Stage 2.

Give yourself time and plenty of opportunity to ride many different horses, and be conscientious in your approach to good yard work and horse management. Good handling of horses with practical, efficient fitting of a wide range of equipment, backed up by sound theoretical knowledge is expected of a good Stage 3 candidate. The Stage 3 rider must be competent and confident to ride horses on the flat and over fences (show jumps and cross-country). You must be able to maintain the level of the horse's work and show ability to ride and lunge horses that may be fit and in competition work. You must be able to work horses correctly and also talk about their way of going.

Examination format

As mentioned, the units of the exam can be taken on different days or on the same day.

The Horse Knowledge and Care section

This section of the exam involves a theory session in a class room, with discussion on such subjects as fitness, feeding and care of the horse at grass. A **practical session** will involve fitting equipment for competition, including exercise bandages. You will also be required to lunge a horse for exercise. A **practical oral session** will cover the horse's physiology with regard to respiration and circulation, the superficial muscles, sites of wear and tear, and 'lumps and bumps' (e.g. splints, windgalls and curbs) and assessing a horse's action when he is trotted up in hand. During all the stable management sections you will be part of a group of up to five, with one assessor per section.

The Riding section

The riding section will involve a session **on the flat** where you will ride two or three horses. Each horse will be in a snaffle bridle and usually a dressage saddle, although some horses may wear general-purpose saddles. After you have ridden one (or possibly more) of the horses, you will be asked to talk to the assessor about how you found the horse. The riding section on the flat lasts around 50–60 minutes, and there will be a group of up to five of you riding at the same time, usually in an indoor school. If you are successful in the flat work you will move on to riding a horse over show jumps and, if successful here, taking another over a number of cross-country fences (six to ten). The show jumping will start with a progressive warm-up, developing over a grid, building from one to three fences. Then the grid will lead into, or be incorporated in, a course of fences which you must ride in good style and balance. The cross-country will be on a different horse to the one you have show jumped. You will have ample opportunity at the beginning of the day to walk the show-jumping and the cross-country courses. This opportunity should not be missed as it is essential to know exactly where you will be riding and what you will be jumping.

In all sections of the Stage 3 exam you should be demonstrating competence and show a degree of confidence and self-belief. The assessor should feel confident that he or she could leave you to exercise a sensible but fit horse, either on the flat, jumping or on the lunge, and that you could look after this horse (and up to three more) capably and with minimal supervision, on a day-to-day basis.

Stage 3 and the PTT

Remember that achieving the Stage 3 exam (Riding and Horse Knowledge and Care) gives you half of the requirement for the BHS Assistant Instructor's certificate. Passing the Preliminary Teaching Test and then completing a portfolio will give you the mandatory requirement for the award of The British Horse Society Assistant Instructor's certificate.

STAGE 3

EQL Level 3 Diploma in BHS Horse Knowledge and Care

> **IMPORTANT:** Candidates are advised to check that they are working from the latest examination syllabus, as examination content and procedure are liable to alteration. Contact the BHS Examinations Office for up-to-date information regarding the syllabus.

 # Syllabus

Candidates must be physically fit in order to carry out yard and fieldwork efficiently, without undue stress and strain. They will be expected to demonstrate competent use of time.

Candidates will be expected to give practical demonstrations as well as be involved in discussion of selected tasks and topics. All work required for Stage 2 should be carried out to an even higher standard of efficiency, and candidates should show a responsible attitude.

General: An increase of responsibility; looking after a number of horses and ponies (up to four) with less supervision; ensuring that horses, stables, yards and fields are safe and in good order.

UNIT 1

Fit Tack and Equipment and Care for the Competition Horse

10 credits / 65 guided learning hours

Unit Purpose and Aims

The aim of this unit is to provide the learner with the skills, knowledge and understanding to fit tack and equipment to horses for competition and to analyse the consequences of ill-fitting or incorrect tack and equipment. In addition, learners will know the procedures for travelling horses to and from competition. They will understand the after care and welfare of the competition horse. They will be able to work safely and efficiently at all times with minimum supervision. Learners will exhibit a level of skill and autonomy required by industry for career progression to a more senior post, or in order to develop further skills necessary for entry into management or a Level 4 qualification.

Learner Outcomes		Assessment Criteria	
The learner will:		The learner can:	
1.	Be able to work safely and efficiently	1.1	Use safe handling and working procedures, maintaining health, safety and welfare of self, others and horses at all times
		1.2	Maintain a clean working environment for self, others, horses and equipment
		1.3	Manage own time efficiently according to industry practice
2.	Be able to put on and fit tack and boots for competitions	2.1	Put on and fit a double bridle
		2.2	Select, put on and fit tack and boots for cross-country
3.	Know and understand how to fit tack for competition	3.1	Justify tack fitted on the horse
		3.2	Analyse the consequences of ill-fitting and/or incorrect tack
		3.3	Evaluate the use of studs
4.	Know and understand the action of a variety of bits in general use for competition	4.1	Identify bits in general use for competition
		4.2	Analyse the action of bits in general use for competition
5.	Be able to select and put on exercise/schooling bandages	5.1	Select suitable equipment, put on and secure exercise/schooling bandages
6.	Know and understand why exercise/schooling bandages are used	6.1	Evaluate the reasons for and against bandaging
		6.2	Explain the consequences of poor bandaging
7.	Know and understand how to care for a horse after competition	7.1	Explain how to cool down a horse following competition or strenuous exercise
		7.2	Describe procedures undertaken following competition or strenuous exercise
		7.3	Explain health care implications for the horse for the following 24 hours
8.	Know the procedures, legislative requirements and qualifications for travelling horses to and from competition	8.1	Describe the checks to be made on vehicles that are used for transporting horses
		8.2	Summarise the equipment to be taken to a competition
		8.3	Explain how to load and unload a horse with regards to safety of self, horse and assistants
		8.4	Describe loading difficult horses to maintain health, safety and welfare of self, horse and assistants

UNIT 2
Horse Health, Anatomy and Physiology
10 credits / 65 guided learning hours

Unit Purpose and Aims
The aim of this unit is to provide the learner with the skills, knowledge and understanding to make evaluations on horse's health, anatomy and physiology. Using the horse in front of them, they will be able to evaluate it's confirmation and how it may affect it's way of going. They will recognise the main superficial muscles of the horse and will understand the structure of the lower limb and foot in order to recognise the causes, symptoms and treatment of abnormalities in the lower limb and foot. In addition the learner will know the structure and functions of the horse's circulatory system and be able to discuss associated problems. The Learner will be able to work safely and efficiently with minimum supervision and exhibit a level of knowledge, understanding and autonomy required by the industry for career progression to a more senior post or in order to develop further knowledge and understanding necessary for a Level 4 qualification.

Learner Outcomes		Assessment Criteria	
The learner will:		The learner can:	
1.	Be able to recognise good and bad conformation	1.1	Describe the horses' proportions with regard to conformation
2.	Understand how conformation may affect a horse's way of going	2.1	Evaluate the horse's conformation and how this may affect it's way of going
		2.2	Describe the 'trotting up' procedure
		2.3	Explain the value of the 'trotting up' procedure in assessing the horse's action
		2.4	Describe the horse's posture and action when lame
3.	Be able to locate the main superficial muscles	3.1	Locate and name the main superficial muscles of the horse
4.	Know and understand the anatomical structure of the lower limbs	4.1	Locate and name the structure of the horse's lower limbs
5.	Understand lower limb abnormalities	5.1	Identify and give the causes, symptoms and treatment for abnormalities of the horse's lower limbs
6.	Understand the principles for shoeing horses	6.1	Differentiate between good and incorrect foot balance for the shod and unshod horse
		6.2	Summarise how the state of a horse's shoes can indicate its way of going
		6.3	Identify problems which may arise from incorrect foot conformation and balance
		6.4	Identify the purpose and characteristics of shoes and pads
		6.5	Describe the purpose of remedial shoeing and welfare implications
7.	Know the structure and functions of the circulatory and respiratory systems	7.1	Describe the structure and functions of the respiratory system
		7.2	Explain the reasons for changes in the horse's respiration rate
		7.3	Describe the structure and functions of the circulatory system
		7.4	Explain problems associated with the circulatory system

Unit 2 continued

8.	Know and understand the treatment of minor injuries and common ailments	8.1	Explain the causes, symptoms and treatment of common ailments
		8.2	Describe how minor injuries can be treated
		8.3	Describe the contents of a well stocked first aid cabinet for horses
		8.4	Describe isolation procedures for horses and when to implement them

UNIT 3a
The Principles of Feeding and Fittening Horses
6 credits / 39 guided learning hours

Unit Purpose and Aims
The learner will understand the value of a balanced diet for horses. They will understand how to manage stock control, ordering, storage and waste disposal of feedstuffs. The learner will also understand how to get horses fit for medium work. The learner will be able to develop further knowledge and understanding necessary for progression to a Level 4 qualification.

Learner Outcomes		Assessment Criteria	
The learner will:		The learner can:	
1.	Understand the composition of food and its value in the horse's diet	1.1	Explain the importance of nutrients in the horse's diet
		1.2	Explain what is meant by a balanced diet and give an example
		1.3	Explain why water is important to the horse
		1.4	Outline the value of grass, concentrates and bulk in the horse's diet
		1.5	Identify issues that may affect a horse's diet
2.	Understand how to organise a feed room	2.1	Explain the organisation of the feed room to ensure health, safety and welfare
		2.2	Explain the management of feedstuffs - storage, ordering, stock control, waste disposal
3.	Understand how to get horses fit	3.1	Explain fittening programmes to get horses fit for medium work
		3.2	Explain the value of using different exercises and gaits for the fittening process
		3.3	Explain how fittening programmes vary for different types of competition
		3.4	Describe exercise routines to maintain fitness levels
		3.5	Describe fitness indicators in the horse
		3.6	Identify issues that may affect a horse's fittening programme

UNIT 3b
The Principles of Stabling and Grassland Care for Horses
6 credits / 39 guided learning hours

Unit Purpose and Aims
The Learner will know and understand about the behaviour, care and welfare of horses when stabled or turned out. They will know about different types of stable yard design and construction and about health and safety procedures and relevant legislation. They will know and understand about the management of grassland and pasture for horses. The learner will be able to develop further knowledge and understanding necessary for progression to a Level 4 qualification.

Learner Outcomes	Assessment Criteria	
The learner will:	The learner can:	
1. Know about different types of stable yard design and construction	1.1	Compare the different designs and construction materials for stable yards
	1.2	Compare different types of drainage and ventilation
	1.3	Evaluate labour saving fixtures and fittings in stables and on yards
	1.4	Explain why consideration needs to be given to the specific placement of certain horses on a yard
2. Understand horse welfare and behaviour when stabled	2.1	Explain how to behave in order to gain a stabled horse's confidence
	2.2	Explain stereotypical behaviour and its consequences
	2.3	Explain ways to control and prevent stereotypical behaviour
3. Know and understand health and safety procedures and relevant legislation	3.1	Summarise current health and safety legislation applicable to stable yards
	3.2	Explain the relevant health and safety legislation
	3.3	Explain the procedure to be followed in the event of a fire on a yard
	3.4	Explain what is meant by the term 'risk assessment'
4. Understand the management of grassland and pasture for horses	4.1	Describe aspects of good and poor grazing
	4.2	Outline an annual plan for pasture management
	4.3	Evaluate cross grazing
5. Understand horse welfare and behaviour when at grass	5.1	Analyse horse behaviour when turned out
	5.2	Analyse the implications for horse welfare when turned out

UNIT 4
Lunge a Fit Horse for Exercise
5 credits / 33 guided learning hours

Unit Purpose and Aims
Learners will be able to safely, competently and confidently lunge a fit horse for exercise with minimum supervision. They will handle the equipment efficiently and be able to adapt their technique to the temperament of the horse. They will be able to utilise relevant exercises to ensure the horse is well exercised whilst maintaining its level of schooling. Learners will exhibit a level of skill and autonomy required by industry for career progression to a more senior post or in order to develop further skills necessary for a Level 4 qualification.

Learner Outcomes		Assessment Criteria	
The learner will:		The learner can:	
1.	Be able to promote and maintain a safe working environment	1.1	Maintain health, safety and welfare of horse, self and others at all times
2.	Be able to lunge a fit horse for exercise	2.1	Use lunge equipment to good effect
		2.2	Lunge a horse to maintain its level of schooling using suitable exercises
		2.3	Use a technique appropriate for the horse being lunged
3.	Understand why and how horses are lunged	3.1	Evaluate the lungeing session
		3.2	Explain the value of lungeing and long reining.
		3.3	Explain the importance of rhythm and balance when lungeing horses
		3.4	Explain the importance of the fitting and safety of the lunge equipment used
		3.5	Explain the benefits of the lunge equipment used

For those of you who have not seen the syllabus in this format before (it was revised in 2011), a little explanation will reassure you that the standards and requirements of the Stage 3 exam are unchanged.

There are now 5 units in the horse care section (including lungeing) and 2 units in the riding section. You will not be permitted to take the jumping unit until you have passed the flat riding unit.

You may enter for all the units together or take them as many as you like at a time, including individually. Should you take more than one unit and pass some and fail others then those you pass will be 'banked' and not have to be re-taken. You will receive unit certification for each unit you pass.

Each unit has a credit value. Each credit recognises 10 hours of work. For example Unit 1: Fit Tack and Equipment and Care for the Competition Horse has a value of 10 credits. This implies you would need to undertake 100 hours of work to be of the standard to pass the unit.

To achieve your BHSAI you still have to compete all the Stage 3 units, the PTT and complete a portfolio.

Remember that all work that was required in Stages 1 and 2 should now be more assured and carried out with greater confidence and to a higher level of efficiency. Candidates should show an increasing awareness of the needs of the horse(s) in their care. They must also show an understanding of the importance of co-operating and communicating with fellow workers. In addition, candidates will be expected to show knowledge and practical ability in the subjects that follow.

Fit Tack and Equipment and Care for the Competition Horse

10 Credits

# Saddlery

Be able to put on and fit tack and boots for competition.

Know and understand how to fit tack for competition.

Know and understand the action of a variety of bits in general use for competition.

Remember that before starting to fit tack the horse must be correctly tied up and the loosebox skipped out.

Tack for cross-country

When fitting tack for cross-country it is necessary to choose a suitable saddle for jumping. Modern jumping saddles have a low cantle and forward cut knee rolls to assist the rider with their fold over a fence and the forward seat required between the fences. Buffalo or rawhide leather are the best for stirrup leathers as they are extra strong. It is best to choose a thin cotton numnah – a thick numnah will only encourage the horse to sweat more.

An overgirth must be fitted to the saddle. This is as an extra safeguard in case part or all of the normal girth should break. The overgirth should sit at the waist of the saddle and follow the line of the girth. Always check on the offside that the overgirth is covering the normal girth and is not too far back on the horse's ribs. The buckle should do up between the horse's front legs through the breastplate loop. If the overgirth is done up at the horse's shoulder it can cause injury, and if it is done up too high it can wreck a rider's boots. Tucked under the breastplate loop there is no danger.

Over-girth done up correctly

Over-girth done up incorrectly

The breast-plate or martingale needs to be put on before the saddle so that it is not necessary to do up the girth twice. If not using a double bridle then choose a bridle with a stronger form of bit and fit it as normal. Ensure that the martingale attachment is fitted correctly to the reins so that the rings 'run' freely. Rubber reins or continental reins are better for cross-country and there must be martingale stops on them if a martingale is attached.

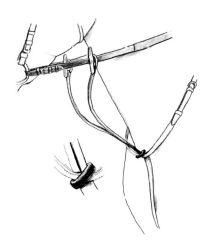

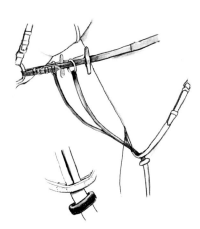

Martingale stops correct

Martingale stops incorrect

Horse tacked up for cross country

The horse's legs must be protected in some way. Many people use some form of brushing boot. These should be fitted to ensure they fully protect the fetlock. There are many different fittings and types to be found these days. If the boots have Velcro fittings then insulation tape should be used to assist with the security of their fitting. As with bandages the tape should not be tighter than the boots. Overreach boots should also be put on. Some riders do not like to use overreach boots as they feel that the horse can tip over should his hind leg catch the boot.

Tack for dressage competitions

A dressage saddle should be applied if asked specifically to tack up for dressage. For a dressage competition a white saddle cloth should be put on under the saddle.

Most people warm their horses up for a dressage competition in white boots. These should have Velcro attachments so they can be quickly removed before entering for the arena for a test.

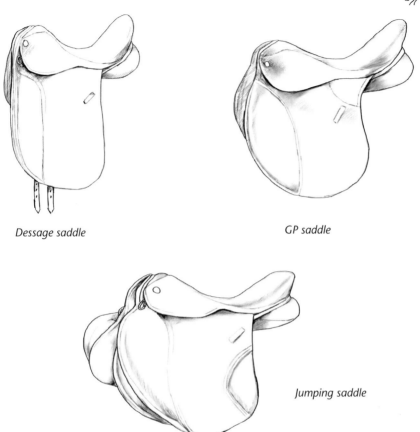

Dessage saddle

GP saddle

Jumping saddle

Fitting the double bridle

To accommodate the second bit in a double bridle there is a sliphead or overhead slip. This is a piece of leather from which the bradoon bit is held. To ensure the number of buckles on the bridle does not become bulky and for general appearance the sliphead is buckled on the offside of the horse's head. This evens up the noseband buckle which is done up on the nearside just as in a snaffle bridle.

When fitting a double bridle always take all the straps out of their keepers and measure the bridle against the horse's head to ensure it is approximately the correct length. Before putting the bridle on untie the quick-release knot and leave the rope through the string and put the headcollar round the horse's neck. It is important that the bridoon is put over the Weymouth so that it can sit correctly when it is in the horse's mouth.

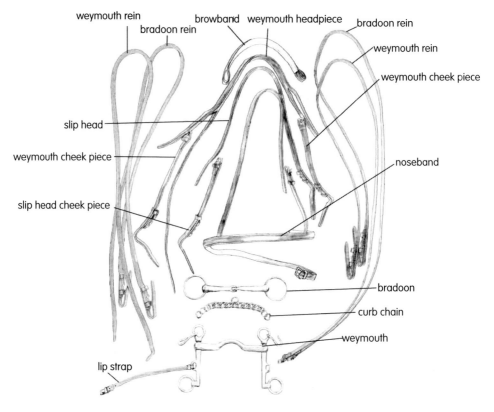

Parts of a double bridle

Make sure that the noseband is well out of the way when putting on a double bridle. It might even be worth holding the noseband up in the right hand with the rest of the bridle leather to ensure this.

Be careful of the horse's teeth when putting the bits in his mouth. When putting on a double bridle the horse may need to open his mouth further than he usually does with a single bit and if he doesn't, there is the potential to knock his teeth. Once the bits are in the mouth efficiently, alter the bits to the correct height. The bradoon should be just a fraction higher than a normal snaffle bit and the Weymouth should lie directly below this. Once they are at the correct height put the leather back in the keepers and do up the throat lash to the usual length (some modern double bridles do not have a throat lash) and the cavesson noseband. Some people like their noseband so that they can easily get a finger in between it and the horse's face, and others prefer it tighter. You may be asked which you prefer and why. A tight noseband can help with some

Double bridle

horses that are resistant in the mouth, but others cannot stand the pressure of a tight strap on their noses and this can restrict them from going forwards, or lead to head tossing and general unsteadiness in the head.

The curb chain should then be done up in the curb groove. It is important that the links lie flat. For the traditional curb chain the links should be turned until they lie flat against each other and the fly link is at the bottom. Then the chain is turned another half a twist and linked onto the hook on the nearside. Some modern weymouth bits have the curb chain hook facing forwards. With these the extra half turn is not necessary. It is important to ensure that the curb chain is not twisted. Traditionally the curb chain is done up tight enough so that when the weymouth shank is at an angle of 45 degrees to the mouth it tightens to the horse's chin groove.

Once the curb chain is done up the lip strap can then be attached through the fly link to help keep it in position.

Usually the reins of the double bridle are of a different width for ease of use. The thicker rein is attached to the bradoon.

Once the double bridle is correctly fitted do not put the headcollar back over it. Many headcollars will not fit safely and comfortably over a double bridle. Take the headcollar from round the horse's neck and hold the horse with the bridoon rein until the assessor comes to talk to you. To do this it is necessary to have completed all the other tacking up exercises first.

Bits

Bits can be split into several different 'families'. There are three main families of bits with a further two groups:

1. snaffles

2. curbs – including the double bridle (weymouth) which also has a bradoon

3. pelhams

4. gags

5. bitless group

A bit can have an effect by applying pressure on the following parts of the horse's head:

- poll

- tongue

- bars

- lips/corners of mouth

- nose

- chin groove

- roof of the mouth

- side of the face

A bit that is accepted by one horse may well be rejected by a similar horse. Although there are accepted ideas such as using an eggbutt snaffle for a horse who likes to mouth the bit and a loose-ring snaffle for one who needs to relax his jaw there will always be horses that do not fit these theories. Sometimes there seems little logic as to why a horse works happily in a particular bit. This is one reason why it must always be remembered that every horse is an individual. If a horse works well in a bit and it is within the regulations if competing in a discipline then utilise it. Any bit is only as good as the hands at the other end of the reins and a supposedly mild bit can be very strong in unsympathetic hands.

Snaffles

Loose ring with thick mouthpiece

Jointed eggbutt

French link

D-ring snaffle

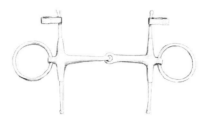

Fulmer (with keepers)

KK

Mullen-mouth rubber

Magenis

Scourier

Happy Mouth

Mouthing

Twisted

Dr Bristol

Cherry roller

Waterford

There is a wide diversity of snaffles on the market today. Generally a snaffle bit has a slight head-raising action. It has an effect on the corners of the horse's mouth, the tongue and the bars. A jointed snaffle will also have a 'nutcracker' action. This puts more pressure on the bars, but allows more room for the tongue. A snaffle that has a double joint helps to relieve some of the nutcracker action. A young horse is usually put into some form of snaffle for his early education and will often work happily throughout his life in this. It is generally easier for a horse to get his tongue over a mullen mouth than a jointed snaffle. A thicker bit tends to be milder than a thinner one, but a horse with a small mouth and/or a fat tongue may well find one too bulky and uncomfortable.

When competing in dressage only certain snaffles area allowed. Generally it is only the 'simple' ones that are permissible but checking in the British Dressage rule book will help to keep readers up to date with any changes.

The double bridle

A double bridle has two bits. The bradoon is a snaffle with small rings and the weymouth is the curb bit which can have a variety of designs, but all have a curb chain. When used with experience and finesse a double bridle gives the rider a greater ease of control and refinement.

A double bridle can be used for horses that have reached a point in their training where they are ready to accept a lighter and more refined aid from the rider. It can also be used in the show ring both for control and appearance. Some riders also use a double bridle when out hunting to ensure they have brakes.

The bradoon acts in a similar way to a snaffle. It can raise the head. The weymouth gives the lighter and more refined aid. It encourages the position of the horse's head as it works towards collection. The influence it has is to encourage the head round and down. It helps with balance and control. The mouthpiece acts on the tongue and the bars and as a fulcrum for the upper and lower cheeks of the bit. When the weymouth rein is used this tightens the curb chain and pressure is applied to the

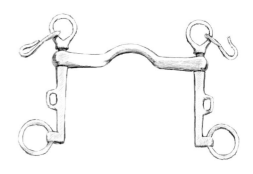

Sliding cheek weymouth

curb groove. The upper part of the cheek piece moves forward and puts pressure on the poll. This means that the longer the shank of the bit the greater the potential severity.

There are several different types of weymouth made from various materials and differing length of shanks, but the most common forms are fixed cheek and sliding cheek.

The rider needs to be able to use each bit independently.

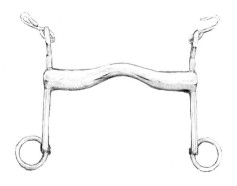

Fixed cheek weymouth

The pelham

This is a 'combination' bit. It is designed to be a 'simple' double bridle. There is one bit which has a shank that has a curb chain and attachments for two reins. Because the two reins are attached to one bit it can have a rather indefinite action. Roundings can be purchased to attach to the two rein slots so that the bit can be used with a single rein. Although the pelham is seen as a compromise bit by many equestrian 'purists' some horses appear to work well in it. Other horses do overbend and try to lean on them.

There are several varieties of pelham mouthpieces : mullen mouth, jointed, vulcanite, rubber are the most frequently seen.

A Rugby pelham is often used in a show ring. It looks a little more like a double

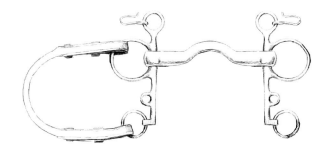

Pelham with and without roundings

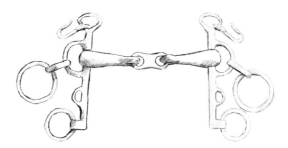

Rugby pelham

bridle, without having the two bits. A kimblewick can be put in this family of bits. A kimblewick is a strong bit that ponies are often being ridden in. A Uxeter kimblewick has extra rein positions within the bit ring making it even stronger.

The Army reversible or universal was designed by the Army for use with as many

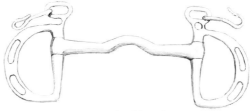

Uxeter kimblewick

horses as possible. It has a reversible mouthpiece that can be either smooth or 'twisted'. It also has 'D' rings for the top rein to attach to and two slots in the shank for the second rein to have a choice of attachment.

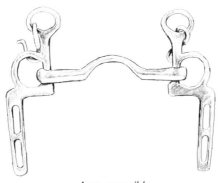

Army reversible

The gag family

A gag could possibly be put into the snaffle family. It does, however, have a lifting action but also applies pressure on the poll. A gag snaffle has two slots in the bit rings through which either leather or cord is threaded. The reins are attached to this at one end and at the other end they are attached to the buckles on the headpiece where the cheek pieces usually attach.

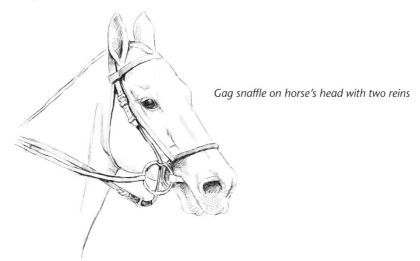

Gag snaffle on horse's head with two reins

A gag snaffle should really be used with two reins. When the rein attached as normal to the bit ring is used then the bit would have the action of a 'normal' snaffle. When the gag reins are brought into play then more control of the lifting action will be obtained. A gag snaffle tends to be used mostly with strong horses that lean when out hunting or going cross-country.

Bitless bridles

A bitless bridle is designed to control a horse by applying pressure on the nose and curb groove. They can be useful for horses who have damaged their mouths and for those who have difficulty in accepting a bit in their

Hackamore

mouths. They are deceptively strong, but can make steering rather vague. There is now a wide range of bitless bridles and the longer the shanks the stronger the action. The original bitlless bridle was called a hackamore.

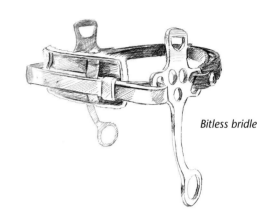

Bitless bridle

Issues with ill-fitting tack

Saddles

If a saddle is too wide at the pommel it can cause sores on the top of the withers and possibly damage the spine.

If a saddle is too long for the horse's back it can put pressure on the kidneys and cause lasting damage.

A saddle that has too much padding will cause the saddle to rock, creating friction and causing a sore back.

A saddle that has uneven padding or a twisted or broken tree will lead to uneven weight distribution. This will cause friction and pressure sores. It will also make the rider crooked, again causing friction.

If the points of the saddle are too long this can put undue pressure on the withers.

Bits

A bit that is too big for a horse's mouth can be uncomfortable, and lead to rubbing and sores.

A bit that is too small can cause pinching and even break the skin of the lips.

A worn bit can again damage the lips or possibly the tongue.

All these will lead to an uncomfortable horse who is unwilling to perform to his best and may even react strongly against the idea of wearing tack and being ridden.

The perfect tack room

A tack room needs to be large enough for the yard that it is servicing. It needs to be sited in such a position that helps with security. If there are people living on site then having it in view or hearing of the accommodation would be useful. If it is sited centrally on the yard this is again good for security. It also helps with accessibility for staff.

It is better for a tack room to be constructed of brick or blocks, again for security. Windows, which should give adequate natural light for working in should be protected with steel bars. Doors should be solid and have secure locking devices. Some yards have a punch number, combination lock on the door for use during the day to ensure that access is restricted only to those who are allowed.

A tack room should have a burglar alarm and external lighting fitted.

Inside the tack room there should be adequate hanging space for saddles and bridles all of which should be labelled with the relevant horse's name. The tack can have named dog discs attached to assist with recognition. There should be access to hot and cold water, and a sink is useful. Heating for staff is always appreciated! Good electric lighting is essential.

There should be plenty of storage room for tack-cleaning equipment, boots, bandages, spare tack, numnahs and bits. Saddle horses and bridle hooks for tack cleaning need to be available. Some yards have an industrial washing machine in their tack room. A fire extinguisher is essential and a notice board is useful for information and horse lists. If first-aid equipment is kept in the tack room then it must be safely stored and marked. Some yards keep rugs in their tack room; others have a separate rug room.

The tack room should always be kept clean and tidy so that both the tack and staff are safe and to create a good impression for clients.

Storing tack and rugs

If storing tack over a long period of time it is best to strip it down and clean it thoroughly. If there are any repairs to be done these should be undertaken. Then either lightly coat it with oil or some kind of leather preserving gel. Place it in a storage bag having first wrapped it in newspaper. This will protect it from mildew. Try and find a place that is warm and safe from vermin for long-term storage.

Rugs should be cleaned and repaired (if necessary) before being stored away. They should then be folded neatly and put either in a large box or heavy plastic container. These should then be put in a clean, dry place that is free from vermin and moths.

There is a section in the examination which is assessed throughout the exam. This section looks at the way in which you show awareness of safety for yourself, the horses you are working around, the equipment you are working with and the others you are working around. Safety is vitally important and by using common sense in all tasks and showing you put safety as a priority you will ensure you will pass this element.

If you are successful in the Stage 3 horse Knowledge and Care you will achieve the Stage 3 Care Diploma. Holding this qualification shows you are competent to take care of a range of horses and should be able to assist with the basic training of students. If you take pride and care in the way in which you turn yourself out you are likely to send a message to employers that you will also take care of the horses you will be responsible for.

You are also assessed on the way in which you utilise the time you are given to complete the tasks. You need to show that you can work at a pace that is acceptable to employers. It is no use being able tack up or turn out a horse perfectly if it takes so long you are unable to complete all the other tasks you have to do on the yard. At a competition a horse has to be ready by a set time. To do this you have to be quick, effective and efficient.

What the assessor is looking for

- You will be expected to fit tack appropriate for dressage and cross-country competitions.

- For dressage you will be required to put on and fit a double bridle and a dressage saddle.

- For cross-country you will be expected to choose a bridle with a bit which might typically be used for cross-country (e.g. a Dutch gag/three-ringed bit, or a Pelham with rubber or laced reins). You may choose a breastplate and/or a martingale, and you will be expected to fit an overgirth.

- You will be asked questions about the fitting of the equipment you have put on. You must be prepared to discuss the implications of ill-fitting or inappropriate equipment. (For example, fitting a heavy quilted saddle pad under a saddle for cross-country would be inappropriate as it is too bulky and hot and has no means of attaching itself to the saddle; ill-fitting tack could cause discomfort or injury.)

- You may have to look at a variety of bits, and these should be familiar to you. Make sure you know which bits are permissible and which are banned in pure dressage competitions. (For example, a double bridle is not permitted until Elementary level and then optional until Advanced, when it becomes mandatory.) Be able to discuss the types of bit which might be used for cross-country riding and for first training of a young horse.

- The assessor is likely to ask you to choose boots appropriate for a specific discipline or for work. You are often asked to fit one front boot and one hind boot. Always choose equipment that is familiar to you and that you have had some experience of using before.

- You may be asked to describe your ideal tack room.

- You may be asked to discuss how to store equipment, including rugs, which may not be in use for a period of time (e.g. storing turn-out rugs during the summer months).

How to become competent

- This is a challenging area of practical competence. You will only achieve competence by frequent repetition, to convey consistency through familiarity in carrying out the tasks.

- If you are not able to fit dressage and jumping saddles in your work placement or training situation, then you must go to a yard where these types of saddle are used regularly.

- Even if you are not regularly able to fit these more specialist saddles, take the time to find some source where you can see them applied and used.

- Always fit a saddle without a numnah or saddle cloth to allow you to see exactly where the saddle makes contact with the horse.

- Get used to managing your equipment efficiently as this indicates competence. Gather all the tack you need and place it close to the stable for easy working. If you have to waste time going back and forth to pick up things you have forgotten (e.g. the girth) you will not convey competence or that you are organised.

- Never leave a valuable saddle in an unsafe place (e.g. on a stable door where a horse could easily knock it off).

- Make sure that you take every opportunity to look at what horses are wearing before and during competitions. Notice:

  - how well the tack stands up to the job asked of it;
  - how well it has been fitted;
  - if poorly fitted, are there any signs of problems (e.g. boots rubbing)?

- Look at the types of numnah or saddle cloth that riders choose for cross-country riding and for dressage classes. If possible, speak to the riders and ask them to explain their choice of equipment.

- Notice the types of rein, bits and boots used for each discipline.

- Look in tack shops and saddlery catalogues to see what is currently on the market for various types of competitive work.

- Ask your instructor to show you how to apply and fit a double bridle and then practise as often as you can. Watch horses working in double bridles in competition. Observe the action of the bits and make sure you are clear on why double bridles are used.

- You must be well practised in fitting a double bridle and know exactly how it is put together and when it is used.

- Be familiar with fitting any type of saddle, though usually a dressage saddle and some kind of jumping saddle is what would be asked for.

- Be familiar with types of bit in everyday use. Ask questions and listen to sound opinions on the action and use of bits. The requirements of the bit are: control/safety/balance and conversation between horse and rider.

- Consider how you would construct your ideal tack room. What would you want in it for the organised, efficient and professional image that you wish to portray? Consider the size appropriate to the equipment to be stored. Think about security, flooring, storage facilities and sources of light, heat and water.

- Be able to discuss the storing of rugs and other equipment which might not be in current use. Consider how this is done in your yard.

- Ask colleagues and friends about the policy they adopt for the storing of rugs and out-of-season equipment.

- Be observant constantly, particularly at competitions, and notice the wide variety of equipment that is in use today.

- Make sure that you have been shown how to fit an overgirth, and that you are quite sure you would recognise the equipment and know how to apply it.

 Clothing

The candidate should be able to:

Select and put on exercise/schooling bandages

Know and understand why exercise/schooling bandages are used.

Exercise/schooling bandages

These types of bandages are used to provide support for tendons and ligaments during work and to protect the legs from concussion and impact. Traditional exercise bandages are made from a cotton and elastic mix and are about 4 inches (10cm) in width. This makes them longer than a traditional tail bandage. They are secured either by tapes or Velcro. Tapes tend to be safer although both are usually secured with electrician's tape or stitched once applied.

Crepe/elasticated exercise bandages should always be fitted with some form of padding between them and the horse's legs. There are several different types of padding; Fybagee, Gamgee and Porter boots are the best known. This padding helps to give more protection and make the bandage more comfortable. Padding made of natural fibres prevents a tendency for the leg to sweat.

Fitting exercise bandages

Firstly ensure the padding is cut to the correct size – the bandage will be applied from just below the knee to just at the top of the fetlock and the padding should be visible both top and bottom.

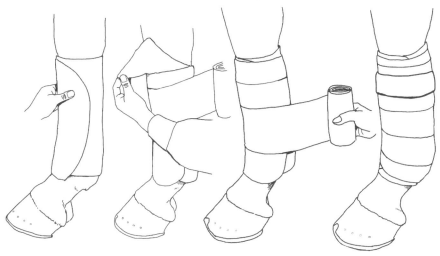

Exercise bandages

The padding should be applied to the leg so that the outer edge faces backwards. This means that on a nearside leg it is in an anticlockwise direction and on an offside leg it is in a clockwise direction.

Holding the padding in place, start bandaging at the top leaving a small flap to turn down. Bandage round the leg once in the same direction as the padding and then turn down the flap and bandage over it. (This helps to secure the bandage.) Continue to bandage down the leg covering approximately two thirds of the bandage already on the leg at each turn. Make sure that the pressure is the same all the way down the leg. Also ensure there are no wrinkles in the padding or the bandage.

The length of the bandage is determined, to some extent, by personal preference. It is, however, generally accepted that you should bandage down to approximately the level of the ergot. Once you have bandaged down to the level required you should return up the leg making an 'inverted V' with the bandage in the middle of the fetlock where the bandage crosses itself to go back up the leg. The pressure should still remain the same.

When the end of the bandage is reached the ties should be kept flat and wrapped around the leg leaving enough length to secure them. They should be tied at the same pressure as the bandage. Some people use a bow, others use a reef knot. Whichever is used the ties should be on the outside of the leg and once secured the top of the last turn of the bandage can be turned down over this for security and neatness. If the

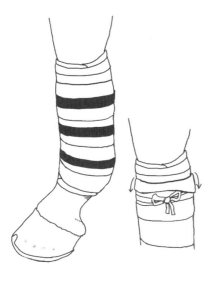

Exercise tape for security

bandage has a Velcro fastening the same principles apply. It can be difficult to turn the bandage down over the Velcro though, as this fastening is thicker than tapes.

If a rider is going cross-country with bandages then further security must be provided. Stitching or insulation tape are the best ways to do this. For Stage 3 the candidate may be asked to tape their bandage. Two or three strands of tape should be put round the bandage at the same tension, one strand being over the ties. If the strands are equally spaced then this looks more professional. The tape should be put on in the same direction as the bandage.

Once completed the tension of the bandage should be checked. To do this insert the index finger in the top of the bandage. There should only just be room for the finger.

To remove a bandage remove the tape and undo the fastening. Pass the bandage from hand to hand as quickly as possible. Do not try to roll the bandage as it is being removed; this will make the operation much slower and the bandage will probably be too loosely and unevenly rolled to be of any use to put back on a leg. To roll a bandage put the ties into small flat loops and roll them into the bandage with the fastening side inwards. It can be useful to run the bandage down your thigh as this can assist in ensuring the bandage is rolled up tightly. If the fastening side of the bandage is not rolled inwards then it will not be possible to tie the bandage securely as it will have to be turned back on itself to be fastened.

If the bandages have been used for cross-country or in a wet/muddy environment they

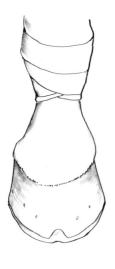

Bandage v shape

will need to be washed before reusing. The padding will also need to be washed, or at least dried and brushed.

There are now many different types of bandage on the market. There are fleece type, inelastic ones that many dressage riders choose to use for schooling. Because of the material they are made of they cannot be applied too tightly and so it is not necessary to put any form of protective padding underneath.

Poorly applied bandages can be extremely dangerous. There is a risk of a bandage coming loose and tripping the horse up. Overtight bandages can cause a restriction in the blood supply to the leg. The risk is enhanced if the bandages get wet (e.g. going through water on a cross-country course) and then dry out again, tightening onto the leg at the same time.

What the assessor is looking for

- You are likely to be asked to apply one or two exercise bandages (or bandages in which the horse could be expected to work/exercise).

- Bandages must be applied with firm, even pressure, and with no increase in pressure when the tapes or Velcro strips are secured to keep the bandage in place.

- You must demonstrate competence and efficiency in applying exercise bandages, completing the task at an appropriate speed.

- You should always show an awareness of your own position in relation to that of the horse in the stable, especially when applying hind leg bandages. (For example, do not position yourself in a tight space between the wall and the horse's hind leg.)

How to become competent

- Exercise bandages are not used extensively these days because of the wide range of alternative leg protection that is available on the market. Because bandaging is 'examined' as a task in the Stage 3, it is essential that you have practised sufficiently to ensure that you are competent and can apply bandages to all four legs in an efficient way.

- If you do not have a horse that is regularly wearing bandages for work, then apply bandages as often as you can (preferably every day for at least a month before your exam).

- Ask someone with greater experience than yourself to check the bandages.

- Look at horses in competition and notice what they are wearing on their legs. If you have the opportunity, watch competition riders applying bandages and notice how firmly they fit them and what padding (if any) they use underneath.

- Seek the opinion of riders, instructors and your vet for their thoughts on the pros and cons of bandaging.

- At some stage in your experience, you will probably apply a bandage which comes loose during work. It is hoped that this occurs when riding or schooling at home, and not at some outing of importance. Be aware of the potential danger of tripping caused by a loose bandage.

- Practise securing your bandages well, making sure that the tapes or Velcro are never tighter than the bandage itself.

- Padding under a bandage should be trimmed to just a few millimetres wider than the bandage itself. Discuss this in an exam, rather than actually cutting the euipment provided.

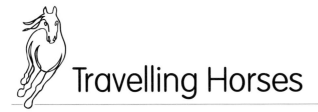

Travelling Horses

Know the procedures and legislative requirements and qualifications for travelling horses to and from competitions.

You may be asked to check a vehicle for safety, and for the horse's safety and well-being, or you may discuss this.

All vehicles need to be regularly serviced. Although this is usually done by a professional such items as checking oil, water, windscreen washer fluid, tyre pressure and tread depth, lights and indicators should we undertaken before each journey. Whether the transport is a lorry or a trailer the ramp and door fasteners should be kept well oiled so they are easy to do up and undo. If the vehicle is a trailer then the hitch must be checked to ensure it is safe.

The vehicle must be taxed, insured and tested (if applicable) and there should be enough fuel for the journey.

Once the legalities have been checked it is important that the area were the horse is to stand is checked. The floor needs to be safe. Wooden floors may well rot over time and this could be disastrous if it gives way when a horse is being transported. Rubber matting on the floor helps to make it non slip and easier to clean, but it may hide a weakness. Even with rubber matting it is better to put a covering of straw or shavings to encourage the horse to stale and to make cleaning out easier after the journey. There needs to be good ventilation, as well as safe partitions and tie rings in the correct places. The roof needs to be high enough so the horse travelling has enough room to carry his head comfortably and is unlikely to hit his head if he throws it up. Solid partitions that ensure a horse cannot bite or kick his neighbour are best.

If the vehicle to be checked is a trailer then also check that the coupling hitch and safety chain are correctly attached.

When checking the vehicle make sure the partitions are placed in the position required for loading the horse. If travelling a single horse on a lorry, he will receive a

Horse tacked up for travelling

better ride the nearer he is to the front of the lorry as he will be affected less by any sway. Make sure the partitions are safely tied back. If travelling a single horse in a two-horse trailer it is better to travel him in the space further from the kerb. The camber of a road will naturally make the trailer lean a little to the left and with a heavy horse on that left side it could encourage the trailer to tilt to the left. Some horses are easier to load onto a trailer if the front ramp is down as well. It makes the trailer look lighter and more inviting.

The situation of the vehicle should also be taken into consideration. If you have a horse that is potentially difficult to load, then putting the vehicle close to a wall on one side may help to encourage him on board. If the vehicle is in the middle of an open space the horse has more places to escape.

Once the vehicle has been inspected you may be asked to check the equipment on a horse that would be travelling. The horse will already be tacked up for travelling. Think back to the Stage 2 practical session where you tacked up a horse for travelling. Discuss the equipment that has been put on the horse. Feel free to ask the assessor any questions you need to, to ascertain your answers. You might want to know how long the horse is travelling for. Is he wearing a leather headcollar and poll guard? Does he have a rug on that is suitable for the weather? (He may not be wearing a rug at all, or he may just be wearing a light summer sheet, both of which could be perfectly acceptable if the weather is hot.) Are his legs well protected? Some people do not like travelling boots and they feel they are less safe than using padding and bandages. His tail also needs to be protected in some way. Discuss these with the assessor and your fellow candidates. If all the equipment is matching and smart then do mention this aspect.

You may be ask what equipment you need to take on your journey and how you know you have got it all. Most people will make a tick list and tick off the items as they are loaded.

What you take with you will depend on the type of competition, the length of the journey, the weather and the length of time you are going to be away.

Some obvious items are:

- tack

- grooming kit

- water

- haynet of hay

- possibly hard feed

- sponges

- sweat scraper

- rugs

- first-aid kit (human and horse)

- studs and spanner

- riding clothes

- food and drink for humans

- buckets

- horse's passport

You may be asked to explain how to load and unload a horse or pony. Make sure you talk about positioning the partitions ready for this procedure in the discussion. You need to talk about working as a team to undertake this exercise and everybody must be fully aware of what their role is. The safety of everybody (including the horse) is paramount.

Anybody involved in loading a horse should be correctly dressed wearing a hat and gloves and, if possible, non-slip footwear.

An assistant should make a final check to ensure that everything is ready and be concentrating on what is going on, available to carry out any instructions. They should stand quietly at the side of the ramp, but not in front of the horse's eye line. This will discourage him from going up the ramp. When the horse has loaded they must quickly and efficiently secure the partition (or if it is a trailer, the breeching strap). The ramp should then be lifted and secured. It is absolutely imperative that when closing a trailer ramp the assistant stands to the side and not under the ramp. If the horse were to pull back and break the breeching strap the ramp could then fall down onto them with disastrous consequences.

If you were to lead the horse it would be better to put a bridle on over the headcollar if you do not know the horse. This will give you more control and the bridle can be taken off once the horse is secure in the vehicle. Do not put the bridle on first and then the headcollar as you will have to take the headcollar off, then the bridle off and then put the headcollar back on once you have loaded the horse.

Lead the horse positively with the reins and headcollar rope in your hands. You may choose to carry a whip in your left hand. Make sure when you lead the horse you do not look back at him – this will 'back him off'. Start a short distance from the ramp and walk the horse positively forward and straight up the ramp. Remember it is the horse that should go up the middle of the ramp, so the leader should be slightly to the left. If the horse hangs back going up the ramp then do not pull him, try to push him past you with a straight arm. The more you pull a horse the more he will pull against you. Once you have the horse safely in the vehicle then the partition can be closed and you can tie him up. If loading in a trailer you will have to be fairly athletic to duck under the breast bar. Whether you are loading in a trailer or a lorry it is always safer to exit via the groom's door.

To unload the horse, make sure that the area is safe for horse and humans. There must be enough room for the ramp to come down and for the horse to exit safely. It is better to enter through the groom's door, talk to and pat the horse. Tell your assistant that they must not undo the ramp and partition until you have told them to. It is better to undo the horse before this happens, so that he does not panic if he tries to get out. Once you have untied the horse you can then tell the assistant to open the vehicle and stand aside – holding the partition open if necessary. You can then walk the horse down the ramp – again making sure he is in the middle of the ramp. Walk away from the ramp and then turn. Do not turn while the horse's hind legs are still on the ramp. If you are in a front unload trailer then the same principles apply. There are very few trailers nowadays where you have to reverse the horse out. If this is the case it is useful for the assistant to put a hand on the horse's rump if he is not walking straight down the ramp. If you have to reverse the horse to unload then do allow him time to walk backwards and think about what he is doing.

You will also be asked to discuss loading difficult horses. It is always better to ensure that a horse loads well before the day he needs to travel and this is done through taking time and ensuring the horse trusts you. You will, however, more than likely come across horses that are reluctant to load. You need to try and establish why the horse is reluctant. He may be genuinely frightened of travelling, the ramp, the small space or have had a bad experience travelling in the past. He may, however, be nappy especially in the yard at home and not be wanting to leave his friends. This may be a sign of feeling insecure because the relationship between the handler and the horse is not strong enough.

Make sure you have the ability to control the horse – a bridle and or cavesson and lunge line will help. Have food and help to hand. You could try putting straw or shavings onto the ramp to make it look more inviting. If the horse refuses to put a foot on the ramp, then having an experienced assistant lift one front foot and then the other onto the ramp may be enough to encourage him to step into the vehicle. Rattling a bowl of nuts in the vehicle or just far enough away from his face that he has to step to eat them may also be just the encouragement that is needed. Make sure that you let him eat the nuts once he is on board though! A person safely positioned behind the horse making a noise (e.g. clapping their hands) may be enough encouragement.

If these simple methods do not do the trick then having two people with lunge lines attached to the vehicle and crossed behind the horse's quarters may help. It is important hat they are not pulled too tight behind the horse as this can encourage his hind legs to come too far under him and he may rear up and lose his balance.

If the handler is positive and experienced this can make a huge difference to the loading process. Being positive and not backing the horse off is very important. Taking time and allowing the horse to trust what is happening will be worth it in the end. Losing your temper and becoming agitated will only lead to a long-term problem that will be difficult to solve.

If you passed your driving test after January 1997 you will need to take a test to drive a vehicle with a weight exceeding 3.5 tonnes. You will also need to take another test if you wish to tow a trailer.

From January 2008 you may need a Welfare of Animals in Transport Order (WATO) Certificate of Competence if you are transporting horses. You will definitely need one if you are transporting horses for hire or reward over 65 kilometres or for up to 8 hours, transporting them for sale or at an abattoir; or as part of your business. You would need to check the Defra website if you were unsure.

What the assessor is looking for

- You may be asked to look at a vehicle (either a trailer attached to a towing vehicle or a horsebox). Often, as a group exercise, you will be expected to check the vehicle for its suitability for transporting one or more horses.

- Be able to discuss the suitability of clothing for travel.

- You may be asked to discuss the type of equipment you would need to take for travelling a horse to a competition.

- It is likely that you will be asked to brief one of the other candidates in your group on the procedure for loading and unloading a horse safely, showing clear awareness for the safety of yourself, the horse and anyone else in proximity.

- You will be asked to discuss how you would assist the loading of a difficult horse.

- You may be asked about current legislation with regard to transporting horses.

How to become competent

- Make sure that you have some knowledge of how to check a vehicle for suitability for travelling horses. The road requirements should be automatic, if you are already a car driver. The horse requirements relate to the safety of the vehicle for horses and their comfort when travelling.

- Look at any horseboxes or trailers that you have the opportunity to see. Whether they be pristine transporters at a local agricultural or county show, or a car and trailer that pulls into the yard in your training centre, take the trouble to look around them and see what features you think are horse friendly or not.

- You should already be familiar in your training or work situation with horses going to competitions. You should be used to equipping them for travelling (Stage 2), and now you may have to look at a horse already dressed and be sure that you are happy that the equipment is appropriate and fitted safely for the journey. Look at as many different situations as you can where horses are

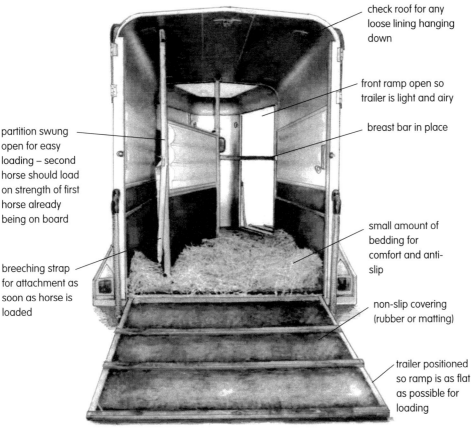

check roof for any loose lining hanging down

front ramp open so trailer is light and airy

breast bar in place

partition swung open for easy loading – second horse should load on strength of first horse already being on board

small amount of bedding for comfort and anti-slip

breeching strap for attachment as soon as horse is loaded

non-slip covering (rubber or matting)

trailer positioned so ramp is as flat as possible for loading

Points to check on a trailer before travelling

travelling, observe what they wear and ask questions where you can as to why a certain rug or leg protection has been chosen.

- Look in tack shops and catalogues at the wide range of equipment available for every type of situation of travelling horses.

- Consider what equipment and supplies would be necessary for even a short journey (e.g. water and haynet). Then consider the extra needs for a longer period away from home (e.g. feeds and extra rugs for an overnight stay). Talk to others who have experience of travelling horses.

- Be able to explain clearly to anyone who may be willing to help you load or unload a horse, what role you wish them to play in the procedure. It is important that whenever you are carrying out loading or unloading everyone involved knows where they are meant to be and what they are doing before starting the process.

- Safety and awareness is of paramount importance, both for horses and handlers. It is always safer, especially with a horse who may be unruly, to wear a hat and gloves for loading.

- Watch as many horses being loaded as you can. Try to observe the procedure in different circumstances (e.g. trailers and lorries). Take note of the methods that may be adopted if a horse is reluctant to load. Consider what measures can be taken to encourage a difficult horse to load or unload.

- Be aware of the possible need to control the horse with greater authority (bridle instead of headcollar or a chiffney to prevent the horse putting his head high to avoid the control from you).

- Assisting loading and unloading horses as often as you can so that you have confidence in maintaining authority over any horse that you are in charge of.

- Consider the best way to secure horses in trailers or lorries. Usually a rope to a piece of string attached to a tie ring in the vehicle is appropriate. The headcollar should be leather, and the rope easy to handle for tying.

- There is no substitute for practice when it comes to loading; it is something that you must do repeatedly, and preferably be as comfortable about loading/unloading a horse into and from a trailer as you do about loading and unloading into and from a lorry/horsebox.

Handling and Time Efficiency

The candidate should be able to:

Work safely and efficiently.

Know and understand how to care for a horse after competition.

Safety and efficiency is subject to continual assessment throughout the examination.

The way you present yourself is important. If you are successful in the Stage 3 Horse Knowledge and Care you will achieve the Stage 3 Care Diploma. Holding this qualification shows you are competent to take care of a range of horses, and that you should be able to assist with the basic training of students.

It is essential you show safety awareness for yourself, the horses you are working around, the equipment you are using and the others you are working with.

Cooling down a horse after a competition or strenuous exercise is vital for his physical and mental well being. Walking the horse with a loosened girth and noseband until he stops blowing will help to ensure his pulse and respiration rates come back down and keep his blood and the oxygen flowing. If it is cold he may need a cooler rug. When he is dry he can be untacked and washed down and offered small drinks of water every 10 minutes. The horse needs to be checked over for injuries and trotted up for soundness. If he is happy to nibble at grass or a haynet that is usually a good sign that all is well

Time handling

This looks at the way in which you utilise time to maximum efficiency.

What the assessor is looking for

- If you take pride and care in the way in which you turn yourself out you are likely to send a message to employers that you will also take care of the horses you will be responsible for.

- Safety is vitally important and by using common sense in all tasks and showing you put safety as a priority is vital.

- You will be assessed on the way in which you utilise the time you are given to complete the tasks. You need to show that you can work at a pace that is acceptable to employers.

- You need to understand why it is important to cool a horse down and how to look after it to ensure its well being.

How to become competent

- It is no use being able to tack up or turn out a horse perfectly if it takes so long you are unable to complete all the other tasks you have to do on the yard. At a competition a horse has to be ready by a set time. To do this you have to be quick, effective and efficient.

- To ensure a horse's well being and continued ability to work cooling him down is an important part of his handling and well being.

- Go to competitions (especially eventing) and observe how the horses are cared for after the cross country phase.

- Make sure you cool down your horse after every work session.

UNIT 2

Horse Health, Anatomy and Physiology

10 Credits

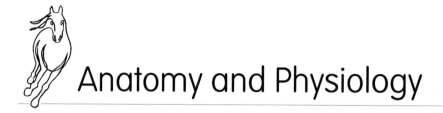

Anatomy and Physiology

The candidate should:

Be able to recognise good and bad conformation.

Understand how conformation may affect a horse's way of going.

Be able to locate the main superficial muscles.

Know and understand the structure of the lower leg.

Understand anatomical lower limb abnormalities.

Know the structure and functions of the horse's respiratory and circulatory systems.

Know and understand the treatment of minor injuries and common ailments.

Conformation

When assessing a horse's conformation it is important first of all to stand back and take an overall look at the horse. If at all possible it may be easier to put a bridle on the horse and take him out of the stable to observe. The candidates will be working in a group and it is important to communicate with one another when looking at the horse so that nobody (including the horse) becomes confused. It is easy for somebody to try and pick up a front leg when another candidate is already looking at the back foot!

Conformation relates to the bone structure of the horse, and the way in which it is put together will have an impact on the horse's way of going and general soundness.

The general impression should be that the horse is built in proportion with no one part drawing the eye. For example if the horse has a refined body and a large head this will be very noticeable when looking at him. The horse's top line should be smooth and well developed. There should be a good, strong looking, sloping shoulder. The back should be short with all four legs set well under the body. The front and hind feet should, as far as possible, be matching pairs.

After looking at the general impression it is best to look at the individual parts, starting at the head.

The **head** should be in proportion to the size of the horse. The way in which the head is set on to the neck can affect the horse's respiration and the ease of flexion. Ideally it should be possible to get a clenched fist between the branches of the lower jaw and at least two fingers between the lower edge of the mandible and the atlas vertebrae. A horse that is 'thick' here may find it difficult to flex.

The horse's **ears** should be relaxed, mobile and of a good size. Hearing is the horse's most important sense. A horse that has big ears is said to have a kind temperament.

The horse's **eyes** should be set wide apart on the head to give good vision. They should have a kind expression and be of a good size. Looking at a horse's eye will tell you a great deal about his temperament. A large, soft eye will usually be the sign of a kind generous horse.

The **nostrils** should be big and wide to allow for an easy intake of air.

The **jaw** should not be 'overshot' (parrot mouthed) or 'undershot'. These are usually hereditary issues that can affect a horse's ability to bite (but not chew).

Overshot jaw

Undershot jaw

The **neck** should appear to come upwards out of the withers. A horse with a low set on neck often has problems with carrying himself 'uphill'. Even if he does carry himself correctly he will never look as 'uphill' as a horse whose neck naturally is more up. If, however, a horse's neck is too up out of the withers it may have issues with becoming genuinely 'round'. The horse's neck should have a concave topline that is muscular. The sternocephalicus muscle under the neck should not be pronounced and bulging. This tends to be the sign of a horse who carries his head too high. The neck should be in proportion to the rest of the body.

The horse's **shoulder** should have a slope of between 45 and 50º from the withers to its point and should appear strong but not overloaded with muscle. An upright shoulder can lead to short, choppy strides.

The **chest** should give plenty of room for the heart, but if it is too wide the horse tends to 'roll' in the canter. If the chest is too narrow the front legs tend to be too close together and the horse is likely to brush.

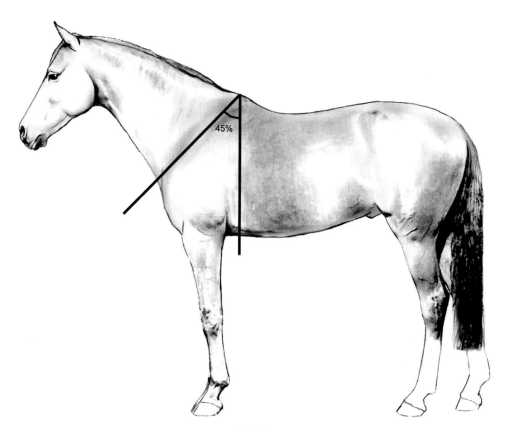

Angle of shoulder

The horse's **back** should be of a length that is in proportion to the rest of his body. If the back is too long then there is a potential for weakness. A long back in a mare is more acceptable as it gives extra room to carry a foal. A short back is strong but tends not to be comfortable to ride. The loins (immediately behind the saddle area) should be broad and muscular.

The body should be deep with well-sprung ribs giving plenty of heart and lung room.

The front **legs** should be straight from the top of the leg to the middle of the foot. If not straight this can put extra strain on tendons, ligaments and joints which can lead to frequent lameness when worked.

A herring-gutted horse

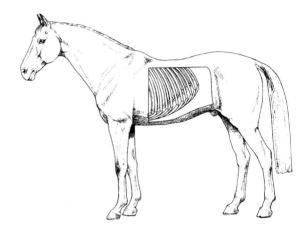

Long in the back

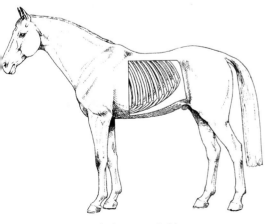

A short-coupled horse

Roach back

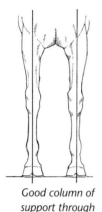
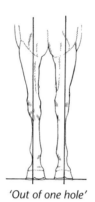
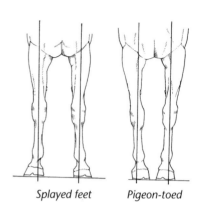

Good column of
support through
centre of limb

'Out of one hole'

Splayed feet

Pigeon-toed

If the horse is tied in at the elbow this can restrict his freedom of movement. The forearm should be longer than the leg below the knee. The shorter the leg below the knee the less potential strain there is on tendons and ligaments because their length will be shorter.

The **knees** should give the appearance of being broad, flat and strong. If the knee appears concave (back at the knee) this can put strain on the tendons. 'Over at the knee' does not put such strain on the tendons and is often seen in older horses that have had a busy life. It is a more acceptable conformational fault.

The **cannon bones** should appear short and strong and not be narrower at the knee than the fetlock. If they are, it is called 'tied in at the knee' and is seen as a weakness because there is less room for tendons and ligaments.

Good knees

Bad knees

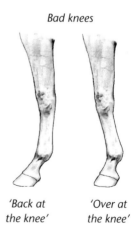

Good column of
support through limb

'Back at
the knee'

'Over at
the knee'

The **fetlock** is the joint, between the cannon bone and the long pastern bone. They should appear large and flat.

The **sesamoid bones** are two small bones at the back of the fetlock. They are pyramid shaped. These bones act as a fulcrum/pulley for the deep digital flexor tendon as it passes over them. The two branches of the suspensory ligament are attached to the sesamoid bones and the annular ligament is bound round the joint to help give strength and support.

The **front pasterns** should appear to be at the same angle as the shoulder (45–50° in the front legs). Long, sloping pasterns tend to give a pleasing, comfortable ride but are liable to strain especially in deep going. Short, upright pasterns tend to give a more uncomfortable ride and subject the foot to more concussion.

The **hind legs** when viewed from behind should show a straight line from the point of buttock, through the hock and the middle of the foot. Looking from the side there should be another straight line that goes from point of buttock, point of hock, down the back of the cannon bone to the ground. The stifle and the hock are vitally important for creating power and pushing the horse forward. Any deviation from correct conformation will mean the horse is highly unlikely to perform to its potential and may well encounter frequent lameness.

The **hocks** should be large with a prominent point. They should be 'well let down'. This means the length from the hock to the fetlock should appear to be short, for the same reason as in the front leg from knee to fetlock. The hind fetlocks should appear flat as in the front legs. The hind pasterns should be at an angle of 50–55°. The hind feet are more oval than the front feet to help with the pushing function of the hind legs.

Superficial muscles

It is necessary to know the names of all the major superficial muscles and be able to pronounce them correctly. It is also necessary to be able to show their position accurately on the horse presented.

The masseter, rhomboideus, splenius, trapezius, sternocephalicus and brachiocephalicus are all in the head and neck.

The deltoid, triceps, superficial pectoral, radial, carpal extensor, common digital extensor and lateral carpal flexor are all in the shoulder and forearm.

The latissimus dorsi, intercostal, longissimus dorsi and posterior pectoral are all in the back or barrel region.

The superficial gluteal, semitendinosus, biceps femoris, deep digital flexor and digital extensor muscles are all in the hindquarters or hind leg.

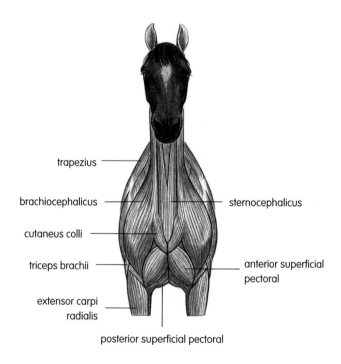

trapezius

brachiocephalicus — — sternocephalicus

cutaneus colli

triceps brachii — — anterior superficial pectoral

extensor carpi radialis

posterior superficial pectoral

Superficial muscles front view

It is useful to understand how muscles work. They work in pairs to move the bones. They are either attached to a bone or are attached to a tendon which is attached to the bone. **Ligaments** attach bone to bone or can help keep a **tendon** in place.

'Bertie Likes Biting My Tiny Bottom' may sound a strange sentence, but it will help you to remember the following – Bone Ligament Bone Muscle Tendon Bone! This should ensure the functions of both do not become confused in your mind.

It is also imperative that the structure of the forelimbs is learnt. The front legs take a huge amount of strain and so have the potential to be easily damaged. Understanding the structure will help to recognise this.

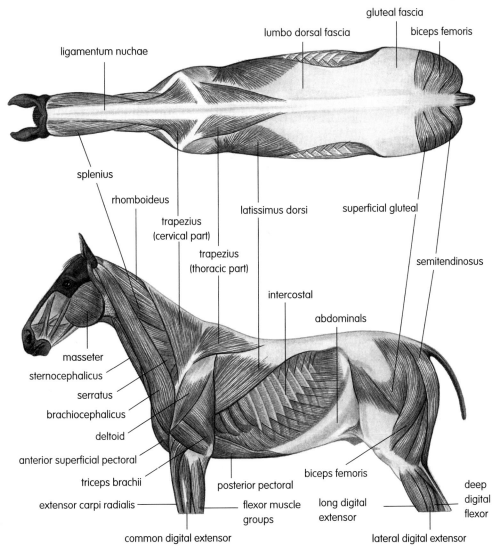

Superficial muscles

The extensor tendons at the front of the leg raise and extend the limb. The flexor tendons at the back of the leg flex the joints.

The **deep digital flexor tendon** (DDFT) originates at the deep flexor muscle. It runs over the back of the knee in the carpal canal and a carpal check ligament helps to

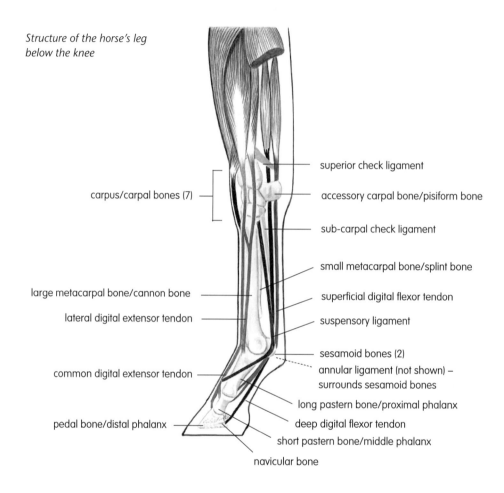

Structure of the horse's leg below the knee

carpus/carpal bones (7)

superior check ligament

accessory carpal bone/pisiform bone

sub-carpal check ligament

small metacarpal bone/splint bone

large metacarpal bone/cannon bone

lateral digital extensor tendon

superficial digital flexor tendon

suspensory ligament

sesamoid bones (2)

common digital extensor tendon

annular ligament (not shown) – surrounds sesamoid bones

long pastern bone/proximal phalanx

pedal bone/distal phalanx

deep digital flexor tendon

short pastern bone/middle phalanx

navicular bone

keep it in position. It extends down the back of the cannon bone and is between the suspensory ligament and the superficial flexor tendon. The inferior check ligament helps with stability and is attached to the tendon approximately half way down the cannon bone. The DDFT then passes over the sesamoid bones and down between the two extensions of the superficial flexor tendon. The tendon then broadens out, passes over the navicular bone and inserts into the lower surface of the pedal bone.

The **superficial digital flexor tendon** (SDFT) originates at the superficial flexor muscle. It runs down the back of the leg, covering the DDFT. At the lower end of the cannon bone it widens and helps to form the annular ligament. Below the fetlock it divides into two and passes either side of the pastern bones. These branches divide again and attach onto the long and short pastern bones.

The **suspensory ligament** originates at the back of the knee and passers down immediately behind the cannon bone. Just above the fetlock it divides. Part binds to make the annular ligament, part attaches to each of the sesamoid bones, and part passes round to the front of the long pastern bone to join with the common digital extensor tendon.

Respiration

Respiration is the system whereby oxygen is taken from the air, passed into the blood stream and carbon dioxide is expelled.

A horse's respiration rate at rest is 8 to 12 breathes per minute.

The respiratory system

- Air is taken in through the nostrils. Horses cannot breathe through their mouths. The nostrils tend to become bigger when a horse needs to take in more air e.g. during fast work. The nostrils are lined with small hairs called cilia which catch dust particles and foreign bodies

- Each nostril has a nasal passage. Air is warmed as it moves up through the nasal passages passing over the turbinate bones. The nasal passages are separated from the mouth by the hard palate. As the palate nears the throat it becomes softer and is then known as the soft palate.

- The nasal passages lead into the pharynx. This is a single cavity through which air passes on its way to the larynx.

- The larynx forms the connection between the pharynx and the trachea. The larynx was designed to protect the lower airways from food and drink. The epiglottis closes and forms a cover over the entrance to the respiratory passages when the horse is eating so that food does not 'go down the wrong way'. The voice box is also part of the larynx.

The respiratory system

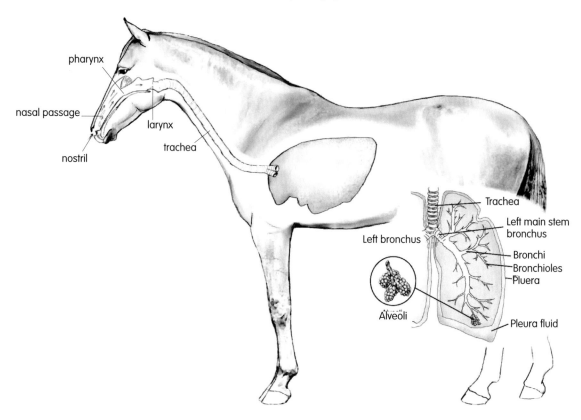

- The trachea or windpipe is made of rings of cartilage held together by strips of muscle. It runs down the ventral surface of the midline of the neck and enters the chest cavity between the first two ribs. It is lined with cilia to help filter the air.

- The trachea divides into two bronchi, one going into each lung.

- Each of the bronchi subdivide into narrower branches called bronchioles.

- The bronchioles continue to divide until they become alveoli.

- The alveoli terminate as alveolar sacs. These look a little like bunches of grapes. They are thin walled sacs covered with capillaries (very small blood vessels). Here gaseous exchange can take place – oxygen is passed into the capillaries and so into the blood stream and carbon dioxide and water vapour are removed and expelled.

The circulatory system

The circulatory system is the transport system of the body. It carries oxygen from the lungs to the body and returns carbon dioxide and waste products.

The heart is a huge muscle that is split into four chambers. The two top chambers are called atria and are for collecting blood and the bottom ones are ventricles for pumping blood. There are non-return valves between each top and bottom chamber.

Arteries carry blood away from the heart. (A good way to remember this is Arteries/Away.) They need to be strong and thick walled as blood is being transported through them by a pumping action. They are capable of expanding and contracting.

The major elements of the circulatory system

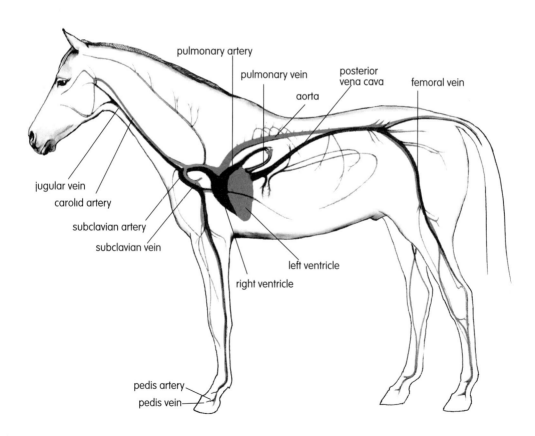

The circulatory system

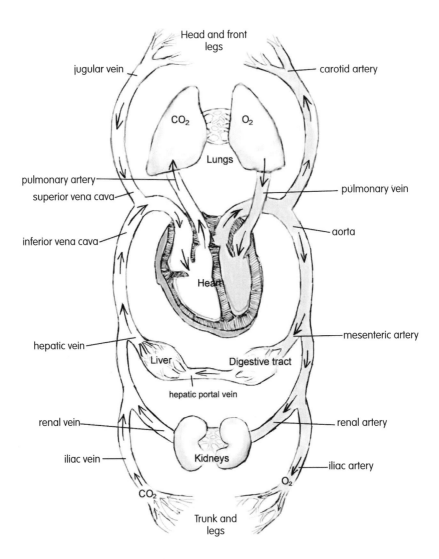

The main artery is the aorta which is connected to the heart at the left ventricle. As the aorta moves away from the heart it divides and branches into smaller arteries and then into arterioles which are small vessels. As they reach their destination in the body they branch even further into capillaries. These are very thin-walled vessels through which fluids and gases can pass into body tissues and waste products can diffuse back. Arterial capillaries lead into venous capillaries.

The heart

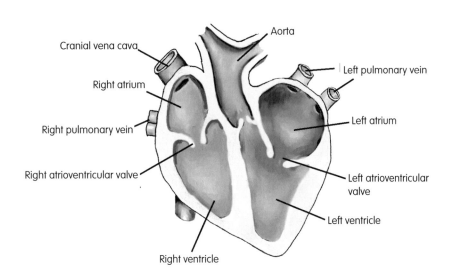

Venous capillaries start to bring the waste products back towards the heart, and as they join together and become a little bigger they are called venules. These venules join together to form veins which all join to make the vena cava which carries blood back to the heart via the right atrium. Veins have valves in them to help prevent blood from flowing in the wrong direction as there is no pumping action as there is in the arteries.

The circulatory system can be split into two: pulmonary circulation and systemic circulation.

Pulmonary Circulation involves the heart and the lungs carrying blood from the heart to the lungs and back again.

Deoxygenated blood enters the heart via the vena cava (the main vein) through the right atrium. It is pumped down into the right ventricle and then to the lungs. Here the gaseous exchange takes place with carbon dioxide and water being exchanged for oxygen. Oxygenated blood then comes from the lungs via the pulmonary vein to the left atrium of the heart. In the pulmonary system the pulmonary artery carries deoxygenated blood and the pulmonary vein carries oxygenated blood.

The **Systemic Circulatory System** consists of the heart and the rest of the body carrying blood from the heart to all other body parts and back again. In the systemic sytem oxygenated blood is carried by the arteries and deoxygenate blood is carried by the veins.

What the assessor is looking for

- This section will be examined in a stable yard, in a group, with up to five candidates at a time working with one assessor.

- A horse will be stood up in the stable, or outside if the weather is good, and the group will be expected to talk about the horse's conformation.

- Conformation relates to the bone structure of the horse. You should first look at the overall picture of the horse and then try to assess the individual parts.

- You should be able to recognise basic good and bad points of conformation, particularly in relation to the fore and hind limbs.

- You may be asked to talk about how you think faults in the horse's conformation might affect his way of going.

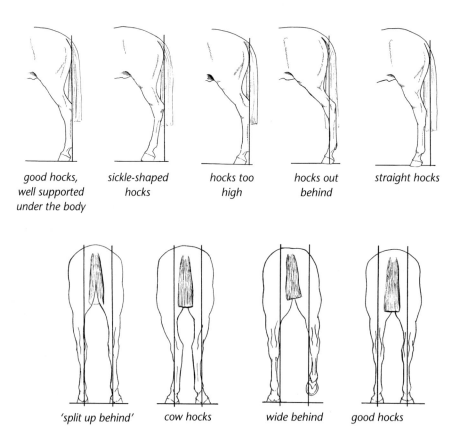

good hocks, well supported under the body   sickle-shaped hocks   hocks too high   hocks out behind   straight hocks

'split up behind'   cow hocks   wide behind   good hocks

Sites of some common ailments

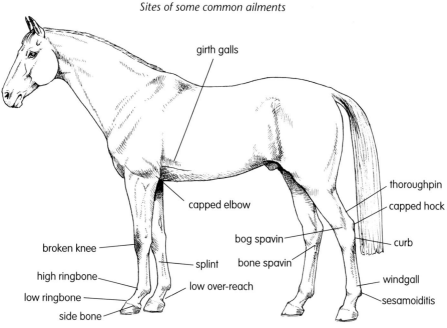

- You will be asked to name and indicate on a horse the location of the superficial muscles of the horse's body and the main tendons and ligaments in the legs. You may also be required to identify and describe the function of the sesamoid bones.

- As a group you will be asked to show where the horse's respiratory tract is, which are the main parts and how these function.

- When asked about the respiratory tract and also about the circulatory system, its parts and function, it is important that you can pick up the discussion at any point, so that you can carry on from where another candidate has stopped.

- You may also be asked how the heart rate can be a fitness indicator. An unfit horse has to breathe faster to supply enough oxygen to his muscles to metabolise into energy. As he becomes fitter his cardio-vascular system becomes more efficient and therefore does not have to work so hard. The heart rate is therefore lower when the horse works and the recovery after work is quicker.

- You may be asked to describe some conditions that arise as a result of circulatory problems. You must be able to talk about filled legs and how you would deal with this condition, and how you might treat acute bleeding, perhaps from an artery, until the vet arrives.

- You will be asked to show on the horse's legs where splints occur. You may be asked about other bony enlargements and you should know where they occur. (Make sure that bone spavin, sesamoiditis, ringbone and sidebone are all familiar to you.)

- You may be asked to show on the limbs where bursal enlargements or soft tissue swellings are found. (Make sure you know where bog spavin, thoroughpins, windgalls and curbs appear.)

- You may be asked to talk about symptoms and treatments of any soft tissue swelling, bursal or bony enlargements and tendon or ligament strains.

- The horse that is presented for this section of the exam is usually one that has plenty of wear and tear on his limbs and exhibits some of the more easily recognised 'lumps and bumps'.

- The horse used for conformation is often one that is not blessed with good bone structure, so it should be easy for you to find some faults.

How to become competent

- When trying to develop an 'eye' for strengths and weaknesses in conformation, you cannot look at too many horses.

- Learn to look at the horse from a slight distance to get an 'overview' of him. Try to recognise the basic proportions of the horse. Does his head match his body for size, does his back look very long or his neck rather short in proportion to the rest of his body? Look more closely at each part of the horse and learn to recognise good and poor areas of conformation.

- Understand terms such as 'upright shoulder', 'over at the knee', and 'cow hocks'.

- Try to look at horses in the presence of someone who is experienced in assessing conformation – this may be your instructor or someone who judges showing classes and has great ability to consider strengths and weaknesses in the horse's build.

- Consider the horse's limbs. Look at the forelimbs from the front and assess the 'column of support', i.e. the way the limb is aligned, by dropping an imaginary vertical (plumb) line from the centre of the shoulder down the front of each forelimb to the ground.

- Look at the hind legs in the same way. Be able to discuss deviations of any of the limbs from the true vertical line and consider how these deviations might put strain on other parts of the limb.

- Consider how weaknesses in conformation might affect the horse's way of going. Speak to your vet and find out what sort of leg injuries he treats and what are the commonest causes of those injuries. Spending a day travelling around with a horse vet can be another excellent way of learning about make and shape of horses, action, injuries and treatments.

- As a competent Stage 3 candidate you should be able to describe the siting of the superficial muscles of the horse with a basic understanding of how they enable the horse to move.

- You must understand the difference between the basic action of a muscle, a tendon and a ligament.

- In the same way as you have learned to identify the muscles, you must learn the main tendons and ligaments in the lower limbs. Be able to name them confidently and also to indicate on the horse's leg where each tendon or ligament runs.

- Be sure that you know where the superior check ligament, the sub-carpal check ligament and the suspensory ligaments run.

- Be familiar with the position of the superficial digital flexor tendon, the deep digital flexor tendon, the lateral digital extensor tendon and the common digital extensor tendon.

- In studying the lower limb it is as well to remember the bones: cannon bone, two splint bones, two sesamoid bones, how the shape of the fetlock joint is formed, the long pastern bone, the short pastern bone, the coffin or pedal bone and the navicular bone.

- It is sometimes interesting to compare the anatomy of the human limb with that of the horse to see how the horse's limb has evolved into a 'one-toed' creature from the original five digits present in our own limbs.

- The points of origin and insertion of the ligaments and tendons should be known, with a basic understanding of how the limb is motivated by the tendons and ligaments in conjunction with the muscles in the upper limb.

- Learn the relevant parts of the respiratory and circulatory systems. You will need to be able to explain (with the horse in front of you) how air is taken into the nostrils, and ultimately into the lungs, what happens in the lung tissue and how air is expelled. From this you must then understand the link between the air taken into the lungs and the use of the oxygen by the body – how oxygen is transported around the body and how waste carbon dioxide is then expelled.

- You should understand the basic difference between arteries and veins, and be able to discuss the structure and function of the heart.

- Remember: you may be asked to pick up a discussion half-way through and this is another thing you must be confident about.

- Always be sure to listen to other candidates so that you can add to or disagree with their statement if you feel there is more to say or an incorrect answer has been given.

- The reason for learning about the horse's systems is to enhance your awareness that a possible problem is arising. By understanding when the horse is functioning 'correctly' it is much easier to recognise any small deviation from normal and take necessary action before a problem develops.

- Be able to discuss basic faults in both the circulatory and the respiratory systems. Faults such as 'filled legs' may be visible on one of the horses you have in the stable management part of the exam. Make sure you have studied why filled legs occur and what you should do to 'manage' them or prevent them developing.

- As your experience develops you are likely to have seen or already taken care of a horse whose legs fill. Thus you should know that gentle activity will usually reduce the thickening.

- Be able to recognise profuse bleeding and know that this may be from an artery. In such cases the vet must be called as soon as possible, as the bleeding may need professional help to stop it.

- Recognise that different methods of improving fitness suit different horses, but the main aim of fittening is to develop the horse's cardio-vascular system so that he can do more work more easily and recover more quickly, therefore exposing his body to less stress.

- Try to learn from others who fitten horses for specific disciplines, e.g. eventing or point-to-point racing. It is valuable to back up your theoretical knowledge with some practical information gained from riders who have actually worked towards or competed in any equestrian discipline.

- Be aware that the speed of recovery of the horse from a short, sharp canter will tell you a lot about his fitness and stamina.

- You will be asked to point out on the horse in front of you sites of injury, lumps, bumps and blemishes.

- Look at as many different horses as you can, preferably with a more experienced person beside you – they can point out things that you may miss.

- Be clear on the type of injury that is likely to occur after working a horse persistently on hard ground (e.g. bony problems brought about by excessive jarring – typically splints, sesamoiditis, pedalostitis, ring bone, or bone spavin). Similarly be aware that soft tissue injuries, strains and sprains are more likely to result from stress in heavy or deep going, or from sudden stress when galloping from hard to soft ground or vice versa (bog spavins, thoroughpins, muscle, tendon or ligament injuries, pulls and strains). Windgalls can arise generally as a result of work stress. They can be associated with hard or soft ground but often arise during the summer when the ground gets a little hard.

- Feel confident that you can discuss basic first aid for any of the problems that you may have already identified.

- Always be prepared to suggest that if, after a limited time of your own 'first aid', there is no improvement in the condition (e.g. after hosing a wound to cleanse it and begin to constrict the blood vessels, the blood is still flowing), then you would call the vet.

- Practise looking at legs for blemishes. Remember to let the horse know you are there, before feeling the blemish to see whether it is soft (usually bursal) or hard (usually bony).

- Always consider the horse's response to your touch: he may be showing discomfort if you apply pressure to a blemish, or he may be just reacting to the sensation (to the pressure but not to pain). To be sure, compare the response to pressure on one leg with an equal amount of pressure on the other leg.

- In most cases the treatment of any injury which causes the horse to be lame is a relative period of rest.

The Horse's Foot and Shoeing

The candidate should:

Be able to recognise good and bad foot conformation and balance.

Understand the principles for shoeing horses.

A horse's front feet are round and the hind feet are more oval. This is because the front feet are designed for weight bearing and the hind feet for pushing.

In considering foot balance the aim is to be able to assess whether the horse takes equal weight across his feet from side to side and similar equal weight from back to front. In this way the horse's body weight will come evenly down all four limbs and distribute over the full weight-bearing surface of the foot.

When assessing a horse's feet firstly look at the quality of the horn. Although this may not seem directly related to the horse's foot balance, if the horn is of poor quality it is unlikely the farrier will be able to keep shoes on the horse and so a regular work schedule cannot be maintained. Brittle horn, old nail holes not closed up, ridges in horn growth should all be commented on in the exam.

The front feet should be compared to see if they are a pair. They should match more or less. As humans our feet are generally not identical and we manage to stay relatively sound; the same is true for horses, but any marked differences, and the consequent potential for unsoundness, should be noted.

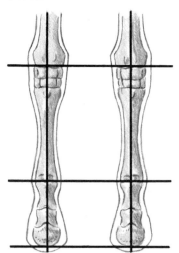

Looking at limb alignment from in front. A vertical line is taken from the front of the shoulder to the ground through the forelimb

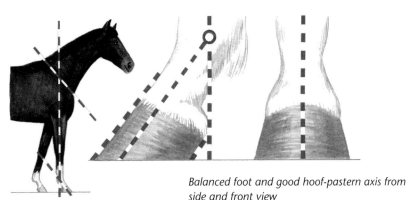

Balanced foot and good hoof-pastern axis from side and front view

Lines demonstrating good balance and alignment of shoulder to pastern angle

The angle of the front foot and pastern should always be related to the angle of the horse's leg and shoulder. These angles should be similar at 45–50°.

When at rest the horse's feet should point directly to the front. If the toes turn in or out this means that the weight put onto the ground is not borne equally over the entire surface of the foot and this can lead to joint and/or tendon/ligament damage.

The hoof–pastern axis (the slope of the hoof and the pastern) should be continuous. Being broken back can again lead to uneven weight distribution through the foot and problems further up the leg including straining of the flexor tendons and the suspensory apparatus. It can also strain the bones and joints.

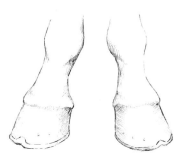

Correct toes   *Toes turned in*   *Toes turned out*

The slopes of the hoof and the pastern being similar will also ensure forward to backward balance. Side-to-side balance is also important because this ensures the foot lands level on the ground.

You may be asked to look at the horse's shoes as an aid to discussing the way in which he moves. Within the discussion always notice and say if the horse is newly shod or   needs shoeing. Any kind of remedial or surgical shoeing should be mentioned. Uneven wear on a shoe will show that a horse consistently puts more weight onto the worn part of the shoe and this is usually symptomatic of an issue somewhere. Worn toes on the hind shoes could simply mean a lazy horse who drags his feet or it could be a joint problem higher up the leg.

Many horses nowadays only work on artificial surfaces and so are unshod. A careful eye must be kept to ensure the surface (especially if it is sand based) does not wear the foot away.

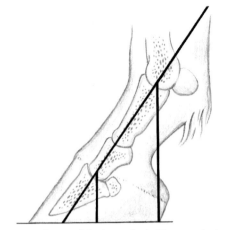

Bones of the lower limb. Lines marked demonstrate good alignment and foot balance

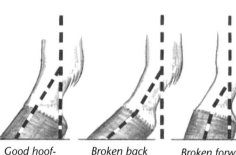

Good hoof-pastern axis

Broken back hoof-pastern axis; puts strain on the back of the leg

Broken forward hoof-pastern axis subjects lower limb and foot to more concussion

What the assessor is looking for

- The key word here is 'observation', and you must be able to describe what you see. There may be a group of up to five of you discussing one horse, and you must be prepared to say what you think and not be affected by what anyone else says: they may be wrong while you are right.

- To be able to identify good or poor foot balance you must be clear on the principles of foot balance and be able to apply them in practice to the horse that you are looking at.

- Look at a similar vertical line from the side down the limb. From these two lines you can see how the horse's weight is distributed over his foot (from side to side and front to back).

- Be able to show where the hoof–pastern axis is and know whether its angle to the ground is likely to induce possible problems in the horse's action.

- Be able to tell approximately how long ago the horse was shod and whether there are indications to its way of going by the wear on the shoes.

How to become competent

- Watch farriers at work as often as you can. Ideally talk to the farriers who regularly visit your yard; ask many questions to enhance your knowledge of this field.

- In studying conformation you should be familiar with looking at the hoof–pastern axis in relation to the angle of the shoulder in the upper limb.

- You should be able to tell whether the shoe enhances foot balance or impedes it in any way (e.g. tight heels on the shoe cause the shoe to 'constrict' the foot, which over a long period of time would have a detrimental effect).

- Be able to recognise an upright pastern and a sloping pastern and consider the possible weaknesses in action that these two extremes may cause.

- Try to feel in your riding, also, the difference in the 'ride' that a horse with upright feet will give you compared to one with a more sloping hoof–pastern axis.

- Never miss an opportunity to look at feet, and pick them up, if possible.

- Get used to assessing the state of horses' shoes. Learn to recognise the signs of a recently shod foot compared to those of a foot that needs shoeing, and consider the amount of wear on the shoes.

- Remember that these days many horses do much of their work on an artificial surface, so their shoes will not show anything like the wear that they would if they were doing daily road work. You may have to rely more on the signs of growth in the foot and the beginnings of the clenches becoming loose, which would tell you that the shoe had been on for some weeks.

- Adopt a policy of looking at horses while they are standing still and trying to decide how they might move. Observe a horse at halt and then, if possible, watch him move. Your initial thoughts about the horse may be reinforced, or you may want to contradict them in the light of seeing how he actually moves.

- Remember that any opinions you may have about how good or poor conformation may affect the way the horse moves, and what this might predispose him to in the future, are pure speculation. It is always wise therefore to 'suggest' that the horse 'might' suffer certain problems. Always cover yourself and be diplomatic; don't make categorical statements.

- In discussing hoof–pastern axis be able to discuss the 'broken forward' pastern and the 'broken back' pastern, knowing what each weakness in conformation may predispose the horse towards.

- Be able to assess limb alignment by looking at the front legs and drawing an imaginary line from the centre of the front of the shoulder down to the ground.

Understand the principles for shoeing horses

The characteristics of a newly shod foot are:

- The foot should be level to the ground.
- The foot should be suitably reduced in length at both the toe and the heel.
- The frog should be close to the ground.
- The clenches should be in a line and not driven into old nail holes.
- The toe/quarter clips should be neatly cut, not too big, and the clip should be neatly bedded.
- The wall should be only lightly rasped.
- The heels of the shoe should be the correct length for the foot; not too long or too short (unless for remedial reasons).
- The shoe should be made to fit the foot (unless for remedial reasons).
- There should be no daylight between the shoe and the foot.
- The frog and sole should only be trimmed as much as necessary.
- The nails should be of a suitable size.
- The horse should be sound when trotted up.

When discussing what you would not want to see in a newly shod foot it must be remembered that some of the methods may be used by a farrier for remedial reasons.

Always discuss matters with them. Farriers are trained carefully over many years and have a wealth of knowledge about horses' feet and foot balance.

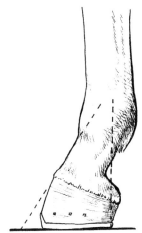

Dumped toe and short heal

- Dumping is where the shoe is set back on the foot and is often too small. The toe of the foot is rasped off to make the foot fit the shoe. The angle of the wall changes as it reaches the bottom of the foot. The foot has a smaller bearing surface.

- Lowering the heels too much puts weight on the back of the foot and so extra strain on the tendons and ligaments. It also means that toes are longer and this can cause the horse to stumble.

- If the sole is pared down too much it could lead to the horse becoming foot sore.

- If the frog is pared away too much it could mean that the horse is unable to work properly. This could lead to increased concussion and/or inadequate blood flow to the foot.

- Rasping the hoof wall too much will lead to the periople becoming damaged. This could lead to the foot drying out and consequent brittleness.

- If the shoes used are too heavy for the horse's foot or for the work he is doing this could lead to overreaching or a possible loss of performance.

- Nail bind is when the farrier has driven the nail too close to the white line and the sensitive laminae and so pressure is exerted. It is rather like getting something between the fingernail and the skin. It hurts and so the horse goes lame. This may or may not show up immediately. It may only cause lameness as the pressure increases.

- Nail prick is where the nail is driven into the white line or sensitive laminae. The majority of horses will show pain immediately and there may be blood on the nail when it is removed. If the horse does not immediately react to the pain, but signs are shown after one or two days pus may well have formed and so the wound will have to be poulticed.

³/4 shoe

Shoe to ease pressure on a corn

Feather edged shoe with spur on outer branch

T bar shoe

Heart bar shoe

Egg bar shoe

- For the exam it will be necessary to recognise a variety of shoes.

- Some pads cover the whole foot; some are inserted between the wall and the shoe and maybe cover the heel region. Some are anti-concussive; and others actually affect the balance of the foot. Some people use a leather or synthetic pad to help minimise concussion and/or to protect the sole, especially in horses with sensitive or non-concave soles. Others say their use is detrimental to the horse as small stones can become trapped under them and the frog is not able to 'breathe'. They can also make the frog and sole sweat. A compromise is the

Hoof pad

type of 'pad' that fits between the shoe and the foot and only projects a small way over the sole. The major issue with these is that it is sometimes more difficult to keep the horse's shoes on.

- Pads fitted in winter can help prevent snow balling in the feet. They can also be used to raise the heel to influence the balance of the foot and reduce pressure on the back of the foot. This, in turn, reduces pressure on the tendons down the back of the leg.

- Studs can be an area of contention. Their use should be discussed with your farrier. Some farriers will only put one stud hole in the outside branch of the shoe so there is less likelihood of the horse damaging the inside of his leg. Other farriers will only put two stud holes in because they feel one stud hole disturbs the horse's foot balance too much. Some high level competition horses will wear four studs in each shoe, two in the heels and one in each quarter of the shoe.

Some riders will not use studs in the horse's front shoes because they feel there is more danger of them being pierced by a front foot stud if they fall off.

Very few people nowadays use road studs. These are small studs, usually in the hind shoes which help to give grip on the road. They are permanent as they are hammered into the shoe. This means that the horse's foot balance is continually disturbed.

The most common form of stud is screw-in. They come in a wide variety of shapes. The general rule is that large, square ones are for wet/muddy going and pointed ones are for hard ground.

Once the farrier has made the stud hole in the shoe and completed the shoeing process it is better to grease the hole and pack it with cotton wool. When needing to use the studs a shoeing nail can be used to take out the cotton wool and a T tap screw used to ensure the thread is clean and sharp.

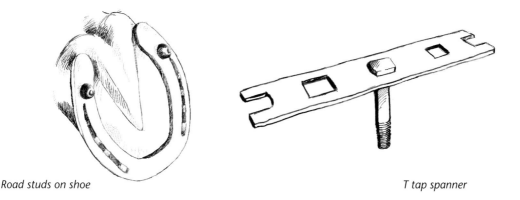

Road studs on shoe   *T tap spanner*

The studs can then be screwed in by hand for the first few turns and then a spanner can be used to ensure they are firmly fitted.

When the horse has finished his work the studs can be removed and the holes re-packed to keep out debris. Ready made plugs can be purchased, but cotton wool is much cheaper.

What the assessor is looking for

- This section is examined in a group, with up to five of you discussing one horse.

- You may be asked to pick up a front or hind foot and describe what you see. The way in which you approach the horse is always taken into consideration, so make sure he knows you are there, particularly before you pick up a foot.

- Systematically describe the foot as you see it. Is the foot a pleasing shape appropriate to the size of the horse; is the horn, at first glance, in good condition?

- On picking up the foot what does the shoe look like? Is it newly shod? Are there signs that the shoe has been on for some time – with the foot beginning to overgrow the shoe, the clenches rising, and the heels beginning to look a little tight? Or is the shoe actually loose and perhaps quite worn?

- You may be asked to discuss what you would not wish to see against the 'ideal' for a newly shod foot.

- There may be a variety of shoes on a table for you to pick out. Be able to identify some of the shoes that may be regarded as 'remedial' or 'specialist' shoes.

- You should be able to recognise if a shoe has stud holes in it, and you may be asked about how to maintain these.

- Understand what types of stud are used for different conditions.

- Be able to recognise pads either in situ on the horse's feet or if handed to you. Understand why and when pads may be used.

How to become competent

- This section requires that you study the work of your farrier carefully and regularly.

- Make sure that you can competently recognise the characteristics of a well-shod foot (e.g. shoe fitting the foot snugly, well-positioned nails, with the clenches smooth and flush with the wall, plenty of weight-bearing surface of the shoe, heels long enough).

- Similarly, be able to discuss features of shoeing that you would prefer not to see (e.g. too much rasping of the wall, the toe cut back ('dumped'), the heels short and pinching).

- In being able to recognise or discuss faults in the well-shod foot, make sure that you can discuss why these faults would be detrimental to the horse.

- Ask your farrier about when he might use pads and how they are fitted between the shoe and the foot.

- Some pads cover the whole foot. Some are inserted between the wall and the shoe and maybe cover the heel region.

- Some pads are anti-concussive, and some actually affect the balance of the foot.

- Some farriers do not like studs, feeling that they affect the balance of the foot adversely; others fit them well forward, away from the heel.

- Make sure that you have looked at the different shapes of studs available for competition work. The chunky, squarer studs are for heavier more holding ground, and the more pointed studs are more suitable for hard ground.

- Make sure that you can identify small road studs, which may be permanently set in the shoes or can be screwed in, to prevent slipping on tarmac. Some people still have a preference for these if doing a lot of road work with their horses.

- If you have never seen any specialist shoes (many of which are not so common today) then study them in a book or try to find someone who can show you some different shoes.

- When looking at a shoe that you do not recognise, work out how it will fit the foot. Consider the shape of it (which should tell you whether it is a hind or a front shoe), consider where the nail holes are and how many there are (e.g. in a feather-edged shoe most of the nail holes will be on the outside of the shoe and the inner edge is tapered or 'feathered' with only a couple of nail holes to secure it, so allowing the shoe to be worn by a horse whose front or hind legs interfere.)

 Action

The candidate should be able to:

Know the sequence of the horse's footfalls at all gaits; good and faulty action.

Describe the 'trotting up' procedure.

Explain the value of the 'totting up procedure' in assessing the horse's action.

Describe the horse's posture and action when lame.

The way in which the horse is handled and how candidates communicate with each other are extremely important. (Candidates should have their hats and gloves to hand for this section).

When taking an unknown horse from his stable, especially to trot up, it is better to put on a bridle. Do not be afraid to ask the assessor if it is acceptable to bring the horse out in a headcollar. If you are asked which you prefer then put on a bridle. There is a very slight possibility of the horse showing bridle lameness, but it is imperative to have the horse under control.

If possible watch the horse as he walks out of the stable. The first few steps might show some stiffness which may have a relation to his action. The horse should be trotted up on a firm, level surface.

Should you be the candidate who is asked to brief the person who is leading the horse then first ask them is they have trotted up a horse for a vet or for inspection before. Then go through the requirements with them. They must walk the horse forward positively, not drag him along. They should walk briskly at his shoulder and not back him off by blocking him with their body or by looking back at him. The horse should be turned clockwise away from the leader and then trotted forward positively using the same principles as in the walk. The leader should be positive and confident but make sure they only have a light contact on the reins so they are not interfering with the horse's head carriage and balance. If the horse is lazy and needs encouragement then you as the organiser should stand a safe distance behind him and give some verbal encouragement.

When watching a horse move make sure it is possible to watch him from the front, back and side. It will be necessary to move to do this. It will not be possible to trot the horse up time after time so make sure you utilise the times he is trotted up by moving around using your own initiative. Also, always listen to the way in which the horse puts his feet to the ground. This will help to distinguish how level, positive and balanced he is.

In any pace the horse should be straight i.e. the hind legs follow exactly the track made by the front legs. The walk should appear as if it is 'going somewhere', demonstrate overtrack, and show rhythm and regularity. The trot again should show purpose, rhythm and regularity.

It is important to watch when the horse is turned. He may well be reluctant to move his hind legs to step under his body correctly. This could be a sign that there is an issue somewhere.

Faults:

Dishing

This is when the foreleg swings outwards from the knee (sometimes from the shoulder). This may be in one or both feet. There does not tend to be any interference to the other leg. It is, however, frowned upon in show classes and does not look particularly endearing in dressage classes. Horses that dish sometimes stand with their toes turned in (pigeon toed).

Dishing

Plaiting

This is also sometimes known as lacing. The horse puts one foot across and in front of the other. There is a possibility that the horse can damage the opposite leg with this movement. Plaiting can occur in both the front and hind legs.

Legs close together

As the horse moves both the front and/or hind legs may come close together. This could lead to the possibility of brushing and consequent injury. Wearing brushing boots will help with this.

Wide behind

This is where the horse's hind legs appear as if they are bowed outwards rather than stepping under the body correctly.

Forging

This is where the toe of the hind shoe catches the shoe of the foreleg. There is a distinctive 'clicking' sound as metal meets metal. Although it is sign the horse is unbalanced, it does also show that the hind leg is stepping under his body.

Plaiting

Overreaching

The hind foot steps into the heel area or pastern of the front foot. This can lead to a nasty wound. It can occur when the horse is jumping or working in muddy going. It can also be exacerbated by a short-coupled horse that takes a long stride. Some people use overreach boots for protection. Others feel that should a horse overreach with boots on there is the potential to bring himself down should he step on the boot.

Speedy cutting

This is similar to overreaching but, because it usually happens at speed, the injury occurs further up the front leg. Speedy cutting boots are longer than brushing boots and are designed to protect from such injuries.

Daisy cutting

This is a straight-legged action often seen in show ponies. The name comes from the fact that the toes are flicked out near to the ground forward and straight. This action has the potential to cut the heads from any daisies, hence the name!

Lameness

The horse presented in the exam will, in all probability, not be lame. If he does appear lame or unlevel in the walk then do not trot him up. It is not fair to trot a blatantly lame horse. There will, however, be a discussion as to how you assess whether or not a horse is lame in front or behind.

If a horse is standing in his box with a front leg pointing or resting in a peculiar way he will often be lame on that leg. If he is resting a hind leg, particularly if he occasionally changes the leg he is resting. Usually this does not indicate a problem.

If a horse is lame on a front leg, in trot he will throw up his head as the lame leg comes to the ground (as if to say 'ouch'). He puts more weight onto the sound leg to favour the lame leg. The lame leg may also have a shorter stride as the horse will try to have as little weight on the leg for as short a time as possible.

A hind leg lameness is more difficult to diagnose. Looking at the hips the sound side may rise higher than the lame side. Again the horse will be trying not to put so much weight on the lame leg. The stride may be shorter on the lame leg.

Always listen to the feet as well. An uneven rhythm may pinpoint the lame leg.

What the assessor is looking for

- Handling the horse well is a priority in this part of the examination.

- You may be asked to 'trot the horse up' as if for inspection for a veterinary surgeon or a prospective purchaser.

- When instructing another person on how to trot the horse up, you must demonstrate your knowledge by the clarity of the instructions you give.

- The horse must be trotted up with competence, efficiency and rhythm. Imagine that a vet or potential buyer is looking at the horse – it is impossible to assess action if the horse is lazy, dragging his feet or losing rhythm.

- Find out where the horse is to be trotted up. Give clear instructions to your assistant so that the horse is presented in walk up to and away from the viewer and similarly in trot.

- If the horse is lazy, be prepared to give some verbal assistance, or put yourself in a safe position where you can encourage the horse to go forward from behind.

- Make sure your assistant is told to turn the horse away from him/her, and to maintain a light contact on the rein(s) or lead rope, not one which in any way could interfere with the horse's natural balance and carriage.

- While the horse is being trotted up, the assessor will want to see you looking at the horse at all times. You can still speak to the assessor without making eye contact. Your eyes must be on the horse particularly during the turn, because here the horse may show an irregularity which is not visible on the flat.

- The assessor will expect you to be able to talk about the horse's action during the 'trot up'.

- You must know if the horse is sound or in any way not completely level in his walk and/or trot.

- Make sure that you have learned terms such as 'plaiting' and 'toe in' and that you understand what they mean. You need to be able to describe the way the horse moves towards you and away from you, if the assessor wants you to.

How to become competent

- Practise trotting up horses: some are easy; others can be sharp and full of themselves. In your exam you need to feel really confident about trotting the horse up yourself or instructing someone to do it for you. This part of the exam is often undertaken badly so it must be practised.

- Look at the way the horse moves, from in front, from the side and from behind.

- Often the horse may have quite different action in the hind limbs as compared to the front limbs.

- Consider the regularity of the gait and also listen to the footfall. Feeling or hearing the footfall will help you recognise whether the horse is taking regular steps or not.

- Be aware of the 'lift' in the steps. Some horses trot up very flat and others show much more spring in their gait. Be prepared to recognise the stiff, but still forward older horse; the full-of-himself younger horse that won't maintain a rhythm; the older 'pottery' horse; and the horse that is actually lame.

- Look at the levelness of the horse's hips as he moves away from you – the level of both sides of the hindquarters should be the same.

- Study the way the feet make contact with the ground. Is the weight taken evenly over the foot from side to side, or does the horse take more weight on one part of his foot than the other?

- Does the foot pick up, travel forward straight, and set down again, or does it deviate in its 'flight path' between picking up and coming down again?

- Make sure that you can lead a horse effectively and that, if briefing an assistant and the horse is lazy or sharp, you are there to assist if he/she is in trouble. Verbal encouragement from behind may motivate a lazy horse, while some reassuring soothing from the handler will usually settle a sharp horse.

Horse Health

The candidate should have:

Explain the causes, symptoms and treatment of common ailments.

Describe how minor injuries can be treated.

Describe the contents of a well stocked first aid cabinet.

Describe isolation procedures for homes and when to implement them.

First-aid cabinet for horses

The contents of a first-aid cabinet for horses will vary from yard to yard, but the following are suggested useful items:

- surgical scissors (blunt ended)
- dressings
- sterile bandages
- thermometer
- Vaseline
- basic wound applications
- stethoscope
- bowl
- vet's phone number should be on the outside of the box

If items are used they should automatically be replaced and one person should be responsible for ensuring everything is kept up to date and complete.

Cold hosing

This is sometimes known as trickle hosing and is used primarily for cleaning small wounds. It is better to grease the horse's heels with Vaseline before starting. Cold water is then trickled from just above the damaged area. This has a constricting effect on the broken blood vessels. It helps to close them and allows the blood to clot. It also helps to wash away foreign bodies and reduce swelling.

Cold hosing can also be used to treat any other leg issues that need cooling.

Cold hosing a leg

Tubbing

Tubbing is used for a foot injury. Again it is advisable to grease the horse's heels before commencing. A shallow bucket or feed bowl is easier to use than a normal bucket. The horse may have to be encouraged to put his foot in the bucket before the water is poured in. The water should not come above the coronary band. Hot water tubbing has a drawing/poulticing effect. If hot water is being used it may need to be replaced. The water should not be so hot that you cannot immerse your hand in it. Cold water tubbing can be used to help clean out small wounds in the foot.

Some horses may not take too kindly to having to stand with their foot in a bucket for fifteen minutes. With the advent of modern techniques and pharmaceuticals tubbing is not used as frequently as it used to be.

Poulticing / hot fomentations

Poulticing can be undertaken warm or cold. Cold poultices are generally used to help ease immediate inflammation and warm poultices help to draw out infection. Warm poultices soften tissue so pus can escape. They also increase the blood supply to the area which assists with healing. It is important that a hot poultice should not be so hot that the heat is unbearable on the back of the hand.

A cold poultice helps to reduce inflammation and helps to constrict blood vessels to help stop internal haemorrhage.

The most common form of poultice nowadays is Animalintex which is a pre prepared product. This can be used hot or cold and instructions for use should be followed carefully including ensuring the plastic layer is in place on the outer side of the dressing. Animalintex should be changed at least every twelve hours.

Kaolin is a traditional product made from a clay mixture. Either heat the whole tin or the amount you need in a microwave oven and then spread on a piece of cloth. As with any poultice it must not be too hot for the back of the hand. It can then be placed on the wound and bandaged into place. Kaolin can also be used cold. It should be left in the fridge to cool.

A bran poultice used to be used for foot problems. It can be mixed with some Epsom Salts if required. The bran is dampened with boiling water. Allowed to cool and then packed into the foot. It then needs to be bandaged and some form of boot (equi

Formenting a forearm

boot or poultice boot) applied or the corner part of a plastic feed sack utilised and tied to the leg.

Fomenting is the application of heat or cold to encourage blood to the area (hot) or constrict blood vessels (cold) to aid healing. Using hot and cold alternately can be beneficial. Small towels are the best items to use for fomentation. Again with the advent of modern pharmaceuticals fomentation is not used as frequently as it used to be.

Colic

Colic is pain in the digestive tract. There are many different possible causes of colic. Some are:

- eating poor quality food
- eating unsuitable food of some kind

- eating too much

- worm damage to the gut

- stress

- a blockage in the gut

- twisted gut

- feeding too soon before or after exercise

- sudden change of feedstuff.

There are many different symptoms of colic. They can be very mild from the horse just being off his food and looking uncomfortable through to the horse lying down, trying to roll, getting up and down and thrashing around violently. He may be sweating and looking at his sides. There may be no droppings or he may have diarrhoea.

If it is felt that the horse has colic then it is important to phone the vet. If symptoms are mild then the vet may not come out immediately, but be asked to be kept updated with regard to the horse's behaviour. If possible the horse should be put in a box with a good bed with high banks to help prevent him injuring himself. Food and water should be removed. If the bout is very mild the horse may improve within about thirty minutes. If not then the vet will come out and try to diagnose the type of colic the horse has. He will often administer a muscle relaxant which may solve the problem very quickly. The vet may well feel other courses of action are necessary depending on the type of colic. Colic surgery, primarily for twisted gut, is now far more successful than it was a few years ago.

Azoturia

Azoturia, sometimes known as tying up, Monday Morning Disease or setfast, is a condition where the muscles of the hindquarters become stiff. This usually happens shortly after exercise has started. The horse becomes reluctant to move forward, is in pain and may start to sweat. The muscles feel hard to touch and may be painful. The respiration rate may increase and if the horse stales the urine may be dark coloured.

Research into azoturia is ongoing. It may be hereditary in certain breeds. It was always considered to be the result of overfeeding without enough exercise – hence the name Monday Morning Disease. In days gone by a horse would hunt on a Saturday, have a day off on Sunday (with no exercise and normal feed regime) and then when exercise started again on Monday the horse may tie up. It is now known that too much glycogen in the muscles creates more lactic acid than can be taken away by blood. The lactic acid is then built up in the muscles and creates the condition. It could be that horses with a selenium and vitamin E deficiency are prone to azoturia. Ongoing research appears to show certain breed types are also prone.

It is important if the horse shows signs of azoturia that work ceases immediately. The loins should be kept warm, even if it is the rider's jacket that is used. Transport needs to be arranged to get the horse home and the vet should be called. The vet may give the horse an anti-inflammatory. A blood test will usually be taken to confirm the diagnosis. The horse needs rest with a laxative diet to recover and should be brought back into work gradually. It is important that the feeding regime of the horse is carefully regulated keeping the hard feed ration to a minimum. Make sure that the horse has some form of exercise every day, even on a day off.

Laminitis

Laminitis is inflammation of the sensitive laminae of the foot. The horse tries to take the weight from the front feet and so stands with his weight resting on the hind feet with the front feet stretched out.

Laminitis stance

There is a reluctance to walk and there will be heat in the feet. Laminitis is generally found in the front feet but may occur in the hind feet.

The most common cause of laminitis is too much rich grass in spring or the second flush in early autumn. Ponies are prone to this condition. Other causes can be concussion, stress and too much carbohydrate from other food sources.

The vet should be called and if grass is the cause then the horse/pony should be removed from the grazing. The vet will usually give pain killers so the horse can be encouraged to take gentle in-hand exercise. The farrier may be called to undertake corrective shoeing/trimming. The horse should be given less nutritious fodder and hard feed cut. There are modern bulk foods on sale specifically designed for horses/ponies that are prone to laminitis and these have been scientifically designed in line with current research. There is a possibility, with severe laminitis, that the pedal bone will rotate and even come through the sole of the foot. To avoid this, quick action should be taken when laminitis is suspected.

Once a horse/pony has had laminitis they are prone to the condition re occurring. Consequently it is important to ensure their feeding regime is carefully managed.

Sick nursing

If a horse is sick it is better to isolate him from the other animals in the yard. His condition may be infectious (spread by air e.g. equine influenza) or contagious (spread by contact e.g. ringworm) and isolating may help to stop other horses becoming ill. Some horses, however, will fret when away from their friends. It is a matter of knowing your horse and doing what is best for him.

Sick-nursing procedure:

- It is better for one person to look after the horse.

- Pay close attention to the horse's comfort, cleanliness and diet.

- Do not fuss around the horse unnecessarily.

- The vet's instructions should be carried out to the letter.

- The stable should be well ventilated.

- The horse should be kept warm with lightweight clothing and stable bandages. If the weather is hot then make sure the horse is not too hot.

- The bed should be deep with good banks. It should be regularly skipped out.

Long straw may get caught round a sick horse's legs and impede his movement. Shavings or paper may be better.

- Do not bother the horse with over-grooming. Keep his feet picked out and remove the stable bandages twice a day to massage the legs and then re-apply them. His eyes, nose and dock can be gently sponged.

- A constant supply of fresh, clean water should be available, if allowed by the vet.

- Feeding should be as directed by the vet. There will be a low concentrate diet. Succulent feeds should be given and the horse tempted to eat by given little and often. Uneaten food should be cleared away. It is important that the horse is tempted to eat and if hand feeding is necessary then time must be taken for this.

- If the horse has an infectious or contagious disease then all tools, grooming kit and equipment must be kept separately. The groom should wear an overall which is kept outside the stable and a bucket of disinfectant must be kept outside the stable door for washing boots.

- Medicine must be administered as per the vet's instructions.

- It is useful to keep a written record of the horse's TPR and general improvement.

Worming

There are a variety of internal parasites that a horse can host. Large redworms, small redworms, roundworms, bots threadworms, pinworms, lungworms and tapeworms are the most common. All horses have a worm burden, but it is essential to keep the amount to a minimum or it can cause anything from unthriftiness to death.

Up-to-date worming techniques have changed traditional thinking with regard to worming a horse. It is now considered cost-effective to have a faecal worm egg count analysis taken and the horse wormed as per the results of this. Traditionally a horse was wormed every six to ten weeks with the wormer being changed so that the horse did not build up a resistance to the drugs being used. A horse was wormed during the winter months with an Ivermetcin-based wormer which kills bots.

Simple rules can be applied to help keep the worm burden down. Droppings should be picked up daily and pasture should not be over-grazed. Cross-grazing with cattle or sheep will help to clear infective larvae. New horses with an unknown worming history should be wormed before being put on pasture.

There is currently a great deal of information on the internet with regard to worming and companies will give free help and guidance in their efforts to gain your custom. The vet will also assist in designing a suitable worming programme for a horse.

What the assessor is looking for

- The information in these elements will be sought through oral questions within the practical oral section of the exam.

- Any riding school or equestrian establishment should have a first-aid cabinet, appropriate for treating minor ailments which may arise and need some immediate treatment prior to the possible later visit by a vet. You may be asked for your ideas on what this cabinet should contain.

- Hosing, tubbing, poulticing and fomentations are all recognised treatments for acute conditions that the horse might suffer from, and the assessor will expect you to have some knowledge and understanding of these.

- You will be asked about the causes, symptoms and treatment of colic, azoturia, and laminitis (and other common conditions). These are all serious but usually avoidable conditions which the horse could suffer from, and you must be able to talk clearly about all three.

- You will also be asked to discuss a sick-nursing regime for an ill horse and an isolation procedure for a horse suffering from an infectious or contagious condition.

- You should be able to discuss worming programmes for horses, including the need for good pasture management as part of a policy for good parasite control in the horse.

- Be sure that you know what worming programme is adopted in the establishment where you have trained and why this system is used.

How to become competent

- As your experience develops you will inevitably see horses that are off colour or ill and horses that suffer an accident or injury and need some basic first aid and management immediately before deciding whether to call the vet.

- Be sure that you take every opportunity to be observant of the day-to-day pattern of behaviour of the horses in your care, so that you notice instantly if this 'normal' behaviour changes as this might be an indicator of a developing problem.

- Symptoms of any condition are always 'abnormal' to the horse's normal pattern of behaviour, so it is essential that you 'know' your horses as well as possible.

- Be able to identify pain demonstrated by your horse. Pain can be manifested in several ways. In a limb or foot the affected limb may be held up or rested excessively, there may be signs of injury, swelling or abnormal stance with a reduced weight-bearing inclination. The foot or limb may be hot, show signs of swelling (in a limb) and the horse may exhibit pain (flinching, reluctance to bear weight or reaction away from light pressure). If there is pain in the gut (digestive tract) the horse may demonstrate restlessness and be inclined to lie down and get up again, as if trying to find a place of comfort. The horse may be off his food and show increasing distress and sometimes violence.

- When a vet comes to treat a horse, make quite sure that you watch what is done and ask tactfully at an appropriate moment what the horse is being treated with. Invite the vet to tell you anything else that is relevant to the immediate treatment or after-care.

- Make sure that you have read up thoroughly on colic, laminitis and azoturia. Try to read *Horse & Hound* regularly as this publication tends to be very up to date with the latest methods of treating horses with these conditions and what the possible cost of treatment might be. (This will vary greatly from one part of the country to another, but you should know what it is for your area).

- Take every opportunity to watch the vet when he is called out to treat a horse in your yard.

- Be able to discuss what you might keep as essentials in the veterinary medicine cabinet. Remember that the contents will be 'past the sell by date' if not used or serviced, so regular checking and updating of the contents is essential.

- Be able to discuss a good sick-nursing regime. Be clear that a contagious condition is one that can only be transferred to another horse by physical contact between an infected horse and non-infected horse. This contact may be as the result of the infection being transferred by an intermediary 'conveyor' (e.g. ringworm spores are transferred from one horse to another through contact, via, for example, tack or grooming brushes used on an infected horse and then again on a 'clean' horse).

- Be able to discuss a worming programme appropriate for horses that are stabled or at grass. Worming procedures vary, but all horses can suffer to some degree from infestation by worms (roundworms, small and large redworms, tapeworms and bots).

- Make sure that you understand the way in which worms act as parasites in horses. Worms use the horse as a 'host', from which they derive nutritional benefit while having a debilitating effect on the horse.

- Eradication is the aim through assessment of the worm burden by an egg count. Treatment with medication to kill the worms and good pasture management to reduce the worm burden on the grassland. This combined approach should maintain horses in good condition, while managing the pasture to the best of your ability and lowering the likelihood of re-infestation.

- Try to find out what worming programme is in place for the yard where you work or train. Discuss the regime with your yard manager or instructor; ask why the programme is used and what worm doses are used, and when, throughout the year.

- Make sure that you have watched horses being treated with a worm dose in a plastic syringe – the dose being given orally. Be aware of the need to check the syringe being used is 'within date' and is sterile at the outset.

- Make sure that you are aware of the need to record the worming procedure and to dispose of the spent syringe in a safe manner where it could not pose a hazard to any animal or human who accidentally picks it up.

UNIT 3A

The Principles of Feeding and Fittening Horses

6 Credits

Watering and Feeding

The candidate should:

Understand the composition of food and its value in the horse's diet.

Understand how to organise the feed room.

Water

Water is essential for life and health. It makes up between 65 and 70% of the horse's body and is lost through natural functions such as urination and digestion, sweating and stress. Horses need between 5 and 10 gallons (20–40 litres) of water per day.

Water is used in:

- Digestion. It is used in the creation of saliva, providing a medium for the transportation of food and electrolytes, and for creating digestive juices.

- Blood and lymph. It is used in the creation of plasma and assisting in moving nutrients and waste around the body.

- Urine and faeces. Waste products are excreted in urine and faeces which contain a high proportion of water.

- Temperature regulation. Excess heat is transferred to the surface of the body and then waste is excreted via sweat.

- The formation of tears and aqueous and vitreous fluid in the eyes.

- Respiration. The formation of mucous in the nostrils.

- Joints. Synovial fluid acts as a lubricant.

- Milk. Water makes up 91% of the milk for lactating mares.

Food and feeding

Food is the source of energy. It is needed by a horse for the maintenance of life, growth and/or work and for the repair of tissue.

Carbohydrates

Carbohydrates are the main source of energy for a horse and should form two-thirds of his feed. Carbohydrates are found in vegetable tissue – plants, grains and grass and are made of carbon, hydrogen and oxygen. There are three types of carbohydrate:

- Starch is the major energy store in plants. It is digested in the small intestine. What is not used for energy is stored in the liver and muscles in the form of glycogen and can then be reconverted to sugars.

- Sugars are the simplest form of carbohydrate. They are also digested in the small intestine.

- Fibre consists of cellulose and lignin. Fibre stimulates the action of the gut and without it the horse cannot digest his food properly. Maintaining a regular intake of fibre allows the horse's digestive system to work as closely as possible to the way it would in its natural state. Fibre consists of cellulose and lignin. Cellulose is broken down by bacteria in the large colon and caecum. Lignin is indigestible for the horse.

If too much carbohydrate is fed it will be stored in the body as fat and make the horse overweight.

Protein

Protein is the body builder. It is essential for growth, repair and replacement of cells and development.

All body cells are made of protein. Consequently young horses and lactating mares require more protein.

Protein is made up of chains of amino acids linked together. Some amino acids can be made (synthesised) by the horse, others are made by micro organisms in the gut and others must be included in the diet. Not all proteins are easily digestible.

Peas and beans, soya bean meal, lucerne and alfalfa are high in protein.

Horses (unless youngstock, lactating mares or old horses) tend to need between 8 and 10% protein in their diets. Working hard may not lead to a necessity for an increase in protein.

A deficiency in protein leads to stunted growth in youngstock, general poor condition and poor muscle development in other horses.

Fats and oils

Fats and oils are important for the growth and maintenance of cell membranes, maintaining body temperature, metabolism of cholesterol, energy and stamina.

All foods will contain a small amount of fat/oil, but traditional rations are very low in oil. Horses are able to digest fat efficiently. Corn oil is digestible and provides two and a half times the calorific value of a similar amount of carbohydrate. Many horses that require a high calorie intake (such as endurance horses and eventers) are fed corn oil as part of their diet.

Minerals and vitamins

These act as catalysts to activate or assist in chemical changes in the body and they are the essential balancers or facilitators that allow the other systems of digestion to operate smoothly.

Vitamins are needed in small amounts and many of them are present in adequate amounts in a correctly fed horse. There are two groups of vitamins:

A,D,E,K are fat soluble and can be stored in the body; B complex and C are water soluble and cannot be stored.

Vitamin A (retinol) is obtained naturally from green herbage which contains carotene which is converted into vitamin A. Carrots and apples also provide a supply. Horses on good grass throughout the summer should have enough stored in their liver for the winter. Vitamin A is important for resistance to disease, and for growth and reproduction.

Vitamin D (calciferol) is produced from the action of sunlight on the skin. A horse living out during the summer will probably have enough stored to last them through the winter. A horse that wears a New Zealand rug or has restricted access to the outdoors may need a Vitamin D supplement. Cod liver oil can supply this. Vitamin D is necessary for the assimilation of calcium and phosphorus. Consequently a lack can cause bone and joint problems.

Vitamin E (tocopherol) is obtained from fresh food such as grain, seeds and green herbage. It is important for the reproductive system and works with selenium. It is also important for muscle tissue and red blood cells. It may help to reduce nervousness in horses. Wheatgerm oil is a good source.

Vitamin K is synthesised by gut micro organisms. It is also found in leafy plants. It is important for blood clotting. However a supplement is not usually necessary.

Some of the B Group complex vitamins are thiamine, riboflavin, folic acid, biotin, niacin, B6 and B12. Some are synthesised in the body and others are found in all food types suitable for horses. They are all important for various enzyme actions. The best known are biotin which is thought to help with hoof formation, B12 with appetite and folic acid which is important for red blood cells.

Vitamin C (ascorbic acid) is synthesised in the horse's body and is found in grass. It is important for maintaining tissues and skin.

Minerals are essential elements but are required in very small quantities. They are inorganic substances. Minerals can be split into macro and micro (or trace elements).

Macro-minerals

- calcium

- phosphorous

- potassium

- sodium

- chlorine

- magnesium

Calcium and phosphorous are the commonest minerals in the horse's body. They need to be correctly balanced in a ratio of 2 parts calcium to 1 part phosphorous. They are important for bone growth.

Potassium is needed for body fluid regulation.

Sodium and chlorine are also needed for body fluid regulation and are lost in sweat. Salt is the best supplement for these.

Magnesium has a major interaction with sodium, chlorine and vitamin D. A lack can cause muscle stiffness and poor performance.

Micro-minerals

- zinc

- manganese

- iron

- fluorine

- iodine

- selenium

- cobalt

- copper

- sulphur.

These all play an important part in enzyme action. They are all found in foodstuffs eaten by horses. A lack of iron causes anaemia.

A balanced diet

A balanced diet provides all the nutrients a horse requires for his lifestyle and in appropriate amounts relative to each other, thus providing a ration which maintains him in an optimum state of health. For the majority of horses/ponies this would be provided by water, hay or haylage and perhaps a small amount of some concentrate food and access to grass.

A horse/pony requires 2½ to 3% of its body weight in food per day. If a horse is going to be fed scientifically then it is important to accurately know his body weight which can be taken by using a weigh bridge. The type of horse, the work he is to undertake, the time of year, his general condition, the rider's ability and the horse's routine must all be taken into consideration when forming a ration.

It is important that the amount of bulk in the horse's diet should be at least 50% of the entire ration even in very hard work. A horse/pony not in work or in slow/gentle work can very easily work off 100% good grass or hay/haylage with no concentrate/hard food.

Some horses may need a small amount (up to 10 to 20%) of hard food for gentle work. In medium level work (being ridden most days with the occasional Riding Club event) a horse may need between 20 and 40% hard feed. Horses tend to be fed too much concentrate food. When talking about feeding regimes for horses it is vey important to remember that each horse is an individual and must be fed accordingly. The basic principles stated above can be used as a starting point.

A 16 hand horse may weigh 500kg (1100lbs). And so would need 2½% of this in feed per day. This amounts to approximately 13kg (28lbs of feed per day). If he is in medium work he could need 25% of his ration as hard feed. This is 3.25kg (7lbs) of hard feed per day.

This could be fed as two feeds per day, and the type of hard feed would depend on the type of work he is doing. For a horse in light or medium work a coarse mix or horse and pony nuts would normally be suitable with a small amount of chaff to add bulk and aid digestion.

When grass kept horses/ponies live out all year their diet needs to be altered relative to the quality and quantity of the grazing, the weather and the work the horse/pony has to do. In spring and late summer/early autumn when the grass is growing access to grass may have to be restricted especially with ponies. This will help to avoid laminitis and obesity. In the winter hay/haylage will usually have to be fed to supplement the grass. A horse living out will probably also need some concentrate feed to ensure he does not lose weight and condition. Ponies may not need concentrate food unless they are working regularly. As with any feed regime every horse must be treated as an individual and their bulk and concentrate food adjusted to ensure their health and condition.

The feed room/store

The feed room should be sited in such a position on the yard that is convenient to reach all the boxes, but is also accessible for delivery vehicles. There should be electricity, hot and cold water, a feed chart, adequate storage for the feed and shelving for supplements and equipment.

The bins for storage of the hard food should be vermin proof. New food should not be put in the bins until all old food is used. If new food is put on top of old food then the old food is likely to go off and taint the new food. It is important to ensure that food is not used after its sell-by date.

The feed room should be designed so that it is easy to keep it clean. It should also be secure so that a loose horse is not able to gain access.

Utensils that are needed for a feed room include:

- feed bowls

- spoons

- buckets

- weighing scales

- scoops

The feed chart should show what each horse is fed for each feed and include any supplements required.

What the assessor is looking for

- The discussion on feeding will be covered in the theory section of the examination, again in your group of up to five candidates. As with all the theory sessions, listen carefully to the answers other candidates give and be prepared to add to or, if necessary, contradict an answer given by someone else, if you think it is incorrect or you can enhance it with more information.

- You will be asked to discuss the importance of water in the diet.

- You will be asked about the value of carbohydrates in the diet.

- You will also be asked about the role of protein in the diet. Make sure that you do not confuse proteins and carbohydrates.

- You may be asked about the role of fats and oils in the diet.

- You may be asked about vitamins and minerals and their value to the horse.

- Be able to discuss the importance of fibre in the diet.

- You will be asked to discuss what is meant by a 'balanced diet'.

- You must be able to discuss why it might be necessary to adjust a horse/pony's diet according to the season and how he is kept (at grass).

- You will also be asked about the amounts of food and ratios of feed you might use for horses in light or medium work or to maintain a level of work. Unless the assessor states what work the horse is doing then ask or create a scenario yourself. It is pointless to estimate amounts of food if you do not know: the size of the horse, the age of the horse, the temperament and type of horse, what work he is doing and perhaps how competent his rider is (and whether he is stabled or at grass).

- You must be able to confidently discuss rations for a horse in your care that does not have access to grass (other than for a brief period of turn-out). In this case he would be dependent on you for all his nutritional needs, and the first consideration must always be the forage ration (in most instances hay or haylage).

- You are likely to be asked how to organise your feed store/room. Consider the ideal in terms of size appropriate to the number of horses.

How to become competent

- Feeding is an art; it comes with experience of looking at horses' condition, understanding what work they are doing and how well they are doing it, and then feeding them accordingly.

- You will find through practical experience that 'hands on' feeding often bears little relation to the rations recommended 'by the book' or by the feed companies, and this is why it is vital to develop an 'eye' for the look of a horse and a 'feel' when you ride him or teach riders on him. It is through this 'feel' that you learn to be able to adapt rations to the horse's individual needs.

- You must, however, understand the concept of how these 'amounts' are calculated so you know where to start with a horse that you don't know.

- The skill of feeding is somewhat reduced these days because there are so many pre-mixed feeds on the market designed to provide nutrients for every type of equestrian activity (e.g. stud cubes for breeding horses, and competition mixes for different disciplines).

- It is still important that you understand what components go into the feeds and what role their nutrients play in the body functions of the horse.

- Read up on feeding as a subject, then study as many different manufactured feeds and their ingredients as you can.

- Collect literature from major feed companies (e.g. Spillers, or Dodson and Horrell). Most food manufacturers produce comprehensive brochures describing the contents and value to the horse of their feeds.

- Talk to your yard manager about what the horses are fed and why.

- Learn to recognise when a feed may need to be changed. For example, if the level of the horse's work is changed; if the horse suffers an injury and has to be rested from work; if the weather changes and makes greater demands on the horse's stamina, old and young horses may need slightly different management.

- Make sure you understand the concept of the ratio of bulk to concentrate feed and ensure that the horse's diet is always at least 50% bulk. For horses in medium work the ratio of bulk to concentrate is likely to be between 80% and 60% bulk to 20% and 40% concentrate respectively.

- Make sure that you have looked at the feed chart in your yard and you know exactly what all the horses are fed and why. Consider the work they are doing and the ratio of bulk to concentrate that they receive.

- At every opportunity be prepared to ask about horses' rations: what they are fed, why they have what they have, what work they are doing and what the feed offers in terms of food value.

 Fittening

The candidate should:

Understand how to get horses fit.

The basic principle of fittening a horse to undertake work is to enable him to fulfil the work required of him with no stress to his limbs, wind or mental state and no resulting damage.

There can be no finite time to get a horse fit for a specific job because there are so many variables. Some of these are:

- the age of the horse

- the type of horse

- whether he has been fit before

- how long he has been out of work

- the possibility of having to take a past injury into account

- facilities available

- time available

- the job the horse is required to undertake

- the possibility of interruptions

- the time of year.

At Stage 2 level a basic fitness programme of six to eight weeks was discussed. Some horses may become fit enough for a Pony Club or Riding Club event in this time, but working on a programme of ten to twelve weeks will probably be more beneficial.

If the horse has been out of work it may be better to undertake certain tasks the week before work actually starts:

- Make sure the horse's vaccinations are up to date.

- Have the horse's teeth checked.

- Have the horse shod.

- Make sure his tack still fits and that it is clean and in good condition

- Bring the horse in each day for a few hours. Give him a handful of hard feed and some hay/haylage.

- If necessary start to tidy his mane and tail.

- Harden the girth and saddle areas with surgical spirit.

- Start grooming.

The programme for the first eight weeks will usually be the same as per the programme used for Stage 2.

The last four weeks of the programme can be used (if necessary) to increase the level of schooling and the amount of fast work.

The success of a fittening programme is dependent on the consistency of the work and the awareness of the rider of any minor problems which might affect the horse's welfare. It is important to check the horse's legs regularly for wear and tear, his enthusiasm, his wind (which will tell you how well he is coping with the faster work) and the length of time it takes him to recover.

Problems and interruptions in a fitness programme will have an effect on the overall time taken to fitten the horse. If he suffers an injury from which he takes time off to recuperate then the time taken for the break must be accounted for within the overall programme.

The weather may have an effect of your fittening programme. Very hot or very wet weather can mean you are not able to undertake the required work. All this needs to be taken into consideration.

The value of different types of exercise

Walking on good going helps to harden and tone up tendons, ligaments and build up muscle without overstressing the rest of the horse's system. It can also help to strengthen bone and help to make it more dense. It is important for the build up of stamina. Consequently the period of walking at the beginning of a fittening programme is absolutely vital as a platform for further work. The rider should not be tempted to make the initial two-week period shorter as injury may be more likely to occur later on in the programme.

Trot work increases the demands made on the horse. Consequently this further strengthens tendons, ligaments and muscles. This improves their effectiveness and enables the horse to start to work more efficiently.

Canter work increases the cardio-vascular efficiency of the body. It also helps increase stamina. Muscles, tendons and ligaments are toned by cantering. It also tends to be enjoyed by both horse and rider!

Riding up hill in any pace makes the horse work harder. The effort required to go up hill is greater than that required on flat going. This makes the heart and lungs work harder thus helping to build up their strength and efficiency. Riding up hill also encourages the horse to use his hind quarters more and so helps to build up his 'engine'. Riding up and down hill also helps the horse to learn how to balance himself, something that is vital if he is going to event.

Short gallops, sometimes known as 'pipe openers' are used to assess a horse's level of fitness. The horse should want to take the rider forwards and be keen and happy to put in the extra effort required. The length of time it takes him to recover will tell the rider whether or not he is fit enough for the task he is being fittened for.

Lungeing is useful to use in a fittening programme once the horse has reached a basic level of fitness in walk and trot. It should not be used at the beginning of a programme as it may put too much strain on the horse's tendons, ligaments and muscles. Lungeing can be used as an alternative form of exercise to help stop the horse becoming bored. It is also useful for the rider to see how the horse is working and how he is moving and how the shape of his body is changing. Lungeing is hard work for the horse and so can also give the rider an indication of how well the fitness programme is progressing by observing his respiration rate, desire to move forward and whether or not he sweats.

Show horses

Show horses tend to be shown with a good covering of flesh. They should not be overweight or heavily topped, although some people tend to put their horses forward in this condition. Those at the top of the showing world are trying very hard to ensure that show horses are not carrying too much weight. Such a horse can suffer joint and leg strain as well as putting undue stress on the cardio-vascular system. Depending on the class entered (and remember there area a huge variety of classes) a show horse does not need to be as fit as a horse competing at low level eventing. However, a show hunter, for example, must be able to gallop without undue strain on its heart, legs and lungs.

What the assessor is looking for

- The questions on fittening will come in the theory section of the examination and you are likely to be asked questions in your group.

- You may be asked about the work appropriate to the first three or four weeks of a fittening programme but remember this will depend a little on where you start from (see 'How to become competent').

- You will be expected to discuss the slow development of the horse's work over a period of weeks to show that you understand the gradual build up of work in walk, trot, canter and then some faster canter work to progressively achieve the fitness required.

- You may be asked about how the fitness of a one-day-event horse may differ from that of a show horse. You must demonstrate an awareness of the different requirements of work of the event horse and the show horse, and this will be reflected in the type of fitness each requires.

- You may be asked about work to maintain the level of a horse's fitness and here again you must demonstrate an understanding of the principles of fittening, followed by sustained work to maintain the fitness level.

How to become competent

- It is quite easy to study books by leading event riders to help you understand the system or method that they adopt to fitten their horses for competition. This can be interesting but may also be confusing, as riders use slightly differing methods to suit their own circumstances.

- Make sure that you take every opportunity to speak to riders who get horses fit for different activities.

- Study horses in different disciplines (even watching racehorses on the television) and what they look like as their fitness develops or when they are fit and competing.

- Make sure you recognise the difference between a horse that is lean, muscled and fit and one that is thin and looking poor.

- Horses involved in any type of galloping work (event horses or racehorses) should always look lean (carrying only enough weight to look sleek and healthy), and not carrying any excess, which would put extra strain on them when they are galloping.

- Show horses, by comparison, are not required to gallop to any great extent and are more likely to carry a fair amount of flesh, which makes them look well rounded and perhaps more 'comfortable' on the eye.

- Recognise that all three basic paces play an equal part in the fitness development. Walk is vital in the early fittening work. Trot work develops stamina and staying power. Working up and down hills increases the horse's balance, flexibility and sure-footedness. Canter develops the cardio-vascular system of the horse (heart and lungs).

- Lungeing can also be a useful tool in the fittening programme and gives you a chance to watch the basic paces of your horse and to see where he is working – or not, as the case may be.

- Once the horse is fit, consider a maintenance programme. Usually a horse does not need to be continually schooled, cantered, jumped day in and out to keep him fit. The maintenance work must suit the horse and your lifestyle otherwise it will become too much of a chore and you will not be able to follow it.

- With the horses that you ride or are involved in looking after, make sure that you are aware of how fit they are.

- Consider the signs that indicate fitness such as: how much the horse sweats or blows after exertion, how quickly the sweating/blowing recovers when you stop the effort, and how tired the horse seems after work.

- Be able to discuss a fittening programme that either you have worked through yourself, or someone close to you has used and you have been able to follow its success.

The Principles of Stabling and Grassland Care for Horses

6 Credits

Stable Design

Know about different types of stable yard design and construction.

Know and understand health and safety procedures and relevant legislation.

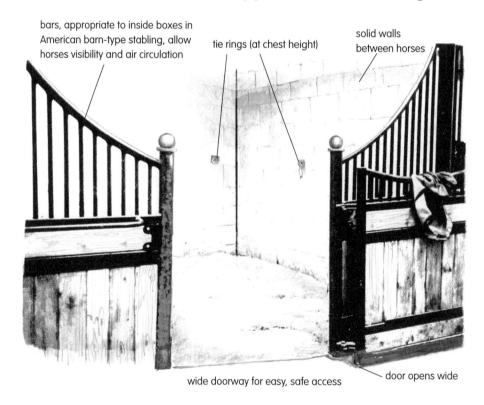

bars, appropriate to inside boxes in American barn-type stabling, allow horses visibility and air circulation

tie rings (at chest height)

solid walls between horses

wide doorway for easy, safe access

door opens wide

A 12ft x 14ft (3.6m x 4.6m) internal stable – a good size. This stable has rubber flooring overlaid with a small amount of bedding for comfort and cleanliness

Candidates may be in the stable yard of the examination centre for this section. Most yards are not perfect but the candidates should start from what they see and say how this differs from what they would like in the 'perfect stable yard'. Although it is better not to be rude about the facilities the candidates should show they know what is safe and acceptable for horses to live in.

A full description of stable design and construction is given in the Stage 2 manual. Candidates are expected to have this knowledge in theory at Stage 2 but at Stage 3 level candidates must be able to adapt this knowledge practically to the facilities around them.

What the assessor is looking for

- You may be asked to look at the stable yard where you are taking your exam.

- Be able to discuss the stables you see against an ideal.

- When thinking of the perfect stable yard, consider the following: size of stables; their configuration (e.g. straight line, quadrangle, or barn style); the materials from which the stables might be made; lighting; ventilation; access; flooring; drainage; and fittings. You may be asked to discuss one or more of these topics.

- For horses, a good size of stable is in the region of 12ft by 14ft (3.6m x 4.6m), bigger is needed for broodmares, and smaller is acceptable for ponies.

- Be able to recognise natural ventilation, and also doors and windows which have been designed to allow good air circulation. Consider the position of windows in relation to doors – it is the flow of air that is important when considering ventilation. A draught over the horse's back is as likely to cause possible health problems as a stuffy stable with poor air circulation.

- You may be asked to look at the stable floor and decide what type of drainage is present.

- Consider whether the stable floor slopes, if it does at all. If it slopes to the back, front or centre then look there to see if there is a corresponding drain.

- Old-fashioned stables often had 'stable brick' floors. These were anti-slip, 'warm' and aided drainage. On the down side, they would now be prohibitively expensive to lay down and labour-intensive to manage (difficult to sweep).

- When asked about the 'traditional stable yard' you should consider how the stables may be sited (in a straight line, or forming a two-, three- or four-sided yard).

- Notice whether there is a concrete 'apron' in front of the stables, an overhang from the roof, and any means of enclosing the stables safely. Be able to discuss the advantages and disadvantages as you see them.

- When considering the advantages and disadvantages of American barn-style stables, make sure that you have some ideas for and against.

- You may be asked about wooden stables, particularly if these are present in the yard in which you are working.

- Wooden stables are reasonably cheap and easy to erect, but they are not hard-wearing, especially if your horses like chewing wood; and they can be stuffy in summer if the ventilation is not good.

- Consider access: doors must be wide (4ft/1.2m at least) and high enough (7ft/2.3m), although it is remarkable how horses can adapt, so comment on this but do not be over-condemning if a horse is living in a stable with a very low access. The chances are he is happy and quite used to it.

- You will be asked to discuss how to choose specific stables for particular horses. Make sure that you can talk about broodmares needing bigger stables, nervous or young horses needing near contact with other horses so that they do not feel isolated, and horses that may thrive more in outside stables rather than in an American barn.

- You are likely to be asked about labour-saving stable fittings. Basic fittings such as tie rings (for tying horses or haynets) are essential for efficient yard management, while the availability of automatic water and fitted mangers is also essential to some people.

Fire procedure

In 2005 new regulations were brought in with regard to fire safety. There is now the need to have a 'responsible person' (a person in control of the premises). One of their roles is to conduct fire risk assessments. The 'responsible person' also has an absolute duty to provide the general fire precautions that are taken:

- To reduce the risk of fire and fire spread

- In relation to the means of escape (MoE) from the premises

- For ensuring that the MoE can be safely and effectively used at all material times

- In relation to fire fighting on the premises

- In relation to detecting and giving warning in case of fire

- In relation to emergency action to be taken in the event of fire, including staff training and mitigating the effects of fire.

Consequently the procedure to be taken in the case of fire will be according to each individual yard's laid down and practised procedures. Generally though, there will be some mechanism for alerting everybody there is a fire, the fire brigade should be called and all persons should assemble at the fire point to check for their safety. If it is safe to do so, horses should be evacuated into pre-arranged fields. The safety of humans must always come first.

Risk assessment

A risk assessment should involve identifying the hazards present for undertaking a task and the extent of the risks.

A hazard is something with the potential to cause harm (e.g. chemicals, horses, ladders).

A risk is the likelihood that the harm from a hazard will be realised (e.g. fall from a ladder, kick from a horse, poison from chemicals). The extent of the risk should also be taken into account i.e. who is affected. (e.g. employee, client, visitor).

In order for the assessment to be suitable and sufficient the following criteria should be satisfied:

- Look at the activity.

- Identify the hazards and risks.

- Ascertain who is likely to be affected.

- Evaluate the likelihood of an accident occurring and the severity of injury or damage.

- Evaluate existing controls i.e. look at what has already been done to prevent an accident.

- Identify any shortfalls and decide what further action is needed to eliminate or reduce the risks.

There are various formulae that can be applied to evaluate the likelihood of an accident occurring and the severity of the injury. One is on a scale of one to three; another is on a scale of one to five. Whichever method is used high and low risks will be identified, and then preventative measures can be put in place to try, where possible, to eliminate or reduce the risk.

Risk Assessments form a very important part of the Health and Safety Policy and Procedures for an establishment and should not be treated lightly. If an accident occurs at a riding school and the HSE become involved, the first thing they will want to see is the Risk Assessment for the task being undertaken.

How to become competent

- You will be familiar with the yard in which you work. Have you tried looking around your yard in an objective way, to see how many advantages and disadvantages you can find?

- You should take every opportunity to look at as many different stable yards as you can. Ask yard workers what they like and don't like about their set-up.

- You can learn from every yard you see. Even visits to trade stands at horse and agricultural shows where stables might be on show can be helpful.

- Most equestrian colleges have an American barn-style stable unit, because for large numbers of horses they are the most economic and labour-saving. If you have no experience of such a unit, make an effort to go and look at one and see how it works.

- In any stable you have access to, look at the floor and see whether there is any visible sign of drainage. There may be a slope on the floor towards a front or rear drain, there may be a central drain with herringbone ridging or a gentle slope taking the wet towards the middle.

- Consider doors, width and access from outside, look at windows, do they open or only provide light, are they protected if they are glass?

- Consider fittings; water systems are all slightly different. How many rings are there? Is there a fixed manger or a manger holder and does this have access from the outside of the stable? (i.e. without opening the door – this would be very labour-saving in a big yard)

- Always consider the yard as a whole. Where is the muck heap? Is the approach up- hill or level? (It's hard work to push wheelbarrows uphill!) What is the yard made of? (Gravel looks smart but is hard to sweep!)

- Talk to people who work in different yards and find out what their likes and dislikes are in the yard in which they work. Looks can be deceptive. A yard which looks super might, in reality, be difficult to manage when you work there day-by-day (e.g. hanging baskets around the yard look lovely in summer, but horses can eat them easily if they are in reach and they take a great deal of watering to keep them looking good).

- Gain as much experience as you can in looking at different stable units and be able to talk about what you see.

Grassland Care

The candidate should:

Understand the management of grassland pasture for horses.

An annual pasture maintenance regime

Winter

In winter horses can inflict a great deal of damage on wet ground. This can lead to poor grazing during spring and summer and an increase in weeds. Many people put aside one or two 'sacrifice' paddocks for winter use. The horses are allowed to 'wreck' these and then they can be repaired and rested in the spring. Fields that are poorly drained should not be grazed during winter. Ponies/horses that live out all winter tend not to damage the ground so much as they are less likely to gallop around.

Spring

When the ground is dry enough it can be harrowed and rolled. If the ground has been poached a great deal it may need to be rolled (to replace the divots) then harrowed and then rolled again. Reseeding can be undertaken if necessary. Reseed poached areas. Ploughing up and reseeding a whole field means that the field cannot be used for grazing for up to a year. A soil analysis can be taken and fertiliser applied as required. Horses must not be grazed on fertilised land until the fertiliser has been washed into the soil by rain. Other things to be checked in spring are the fences and the water troughs.

Any repairs must be undertaken before horses are turned out and the water troughs will need emptying out and scrubbing. During spring weeds need to be kept down. If they are to be sprayed then May is the best time for this. Again horses should not be grazed on land that has been sprayed. As the new grass comes through then ponies may need to be limited on the amount they are allowed to eat. A large field could be divided into three sections and rotational grazing undertaken; one could be grazed by the horses, one rested and one grazed by sheep or cattle. They can be rotated approximately every three weeks.

Summer

During the summer rotational grazing can continue. Droppings should be picked up daily. Topping can be undertaken if necessary. If the field is not being grazed because hay/haylage is going to be cropped, this will be taken in June or July. It is sometimes difficult to get a contractor to find the time to take a crop from a small acreage during their busy season. A contractor may not come when he is required and the grass may be beyond its best when he has the time to take the crop. Weeds need to be kept in check during the summer and ragwort needs to be pulled and burned. Fields can be harrowed regularly throughout the summer.

Autumn

There is a flush of grass during the autumn and this must be managed especially if ponies are being grazed. Fertiliser can be applied in the autumn if necessary. If farm yard manure (FYM) is to be applied this is done in the autumn to allow it to break down during the winter. Acorns need to be dealt with as they are poisonous to horses. Drainage ditches will need to be cleared from the perimeter of the field to help with winter drainage.

A pony will live happily on one acre that is well managed. A horse will need one-and-a-half to two acres if they live out all year round. If pasture is over-grazed it will deteriorate and the quality of grazing will be poor. Weeds will become prolific and there may be a heavy worm burden.

Good quality, palatable grasses need to be encouraged. Some good grasses are:-

| Rye grass | Timothy | Smooth meadow grass | Tall fescue |

Harrowing

Chain harrows remove dead grass and moss helping new growth. Harrows with spikes can help to aerate the ground and again assist with new growth.

Rolling

The pressure of the roller on the ground can help to level the surface of the field. This can make it safer for horses to graze and also ensure more grass growth. The pressure also pushes the roots into the soil and helps them to multiply. It can also discourage weeds.

Fertilising

Fertiliser can hugely improve the quality and quantity of the sward. A soil analysis should be undertaken so that the correct fertiliser is used to aid improvement. Organic fertiliser comes from natural sources such as seaweed or farm yard manure. They are more expensive, but are generally considered to be better for the land. Compound fertilisers usually contain nitrogen, phosphorous and potassium. Too much nitrogen is not good for horses as it makes the grass very lush. Lime needs to be added if the soil has a low pH level. A pH level of 6.5 is suitable for good grass growth.

Topping

It may be necessary from June onwards to 'top' the fields. This is using a cutter designed especially for the task. Topping keeps unpalatable grass from taking over and encourages sweeter grasses to grow. Topping can also help to keep weeds at bay. If paddocks are cross-grazed with sheep or cattle then topping is not usually necessary because they will eat the courser grasses. Cattle and sheep will also ingest worm larvae that use horses as their host.

What the assessor is looking for

- This will be examined in the theory session of the exam, so the questions will be oral in discussion.
- You may be asked to describe how pasture might be managed for horses over a period of a year.

- Be able to discuss the pros and cons of taking hay from a small acreage. A disadvantage is that often it is difficult to ensure a good quality crop. An advantage is that it can be cheaper to make your own hay.

- Be able to talk about maintaining fencing in good order, topping pasture if necessary, and management of weeds – especially the eradication of ragwort.

- You may be asked specifically about harrowing, rolling, topping and fertilising and also about cross-grazing the pasture with other animals, such as sheep or cattle.

- You will also be expected to discuss the approximate acreage which would be the minimum acceptable on which to keep a horse.

- Bear in mind that the principle of one horse/pony per acre is not really appropriate (it would be almost impossible to sustain one pony/horse all year around on only one acre). But as the numbers go up, it is easier to manage the pasture to sustain the number of equines (i.e. four ponies/horses on four acres would be manageable, because paddocks could be set up in rotation).

- The assessor will expect you to be able to discuss the basic management of pasture at any time of the year. It is probably easiest to think of the year month by month in terms of what might be carried out on the land to maintain it, but you must be able to pick up the discussion at any point in the year.

How to become competent

- If you are working in an establishment that has an acreage of land which is used for the horse, be sure to ask about the pasture management and observe the procedures carried out.

- Generally pasture that is used only for horses has some special considerations to take into account. Horses are extremely selective in their grazing habits and if pasture is heavily grazed by horses, it is easy for it to become 'horse-sick'. Horse-sick pasture is identified by areas of apparently 'lawn-like' grazing interspersed with patches of rank long grass where the horses have soiled and then avoided grazing.

- Make a point of watching how pasture is rolled, harrowed, topped and fertilised. Ask the contractor about the type of fertiliser being used.

- It will also be necessary to be aware of the need to manage weeds such as docks, thistles and particularly any influx of ragwort.

- When discussing cross-grazing, be able to compare the benefits of sheep over cattle, or vice versa. Sheep are easier to manage but need low fencing (which might involve wire) to contain them, and they take the grass lower than horses can graze. Cattle, however, sweeten the grassland more with their manure and have an eradicating effect on most horse parasites, but they can be damaging to fencing and any jumps that might be in the field and generally are more unruly to manage.

- Be quite clear in your mind of what a year's basic programme of work to maintain pasture would involve.

- Be able to talk about minimum acreage with regard to managing perhaps six acres with six horses/ponies grazing on this land. You would need to be able to discuss a method of splitting up the pasture into at least two and possibly three paddocks, so that at any time you had the horses grazing one paddock while the other two were resting or perhaps being treated for improvement.

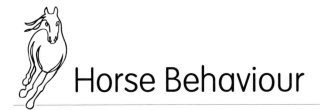

Horse Behaviour

The candidate should:

Understand horse welfare and behaviour at grass.

Understand horse welfare and behaviour when stabled.

Horses in fields

A group of horses living together will sort out their own pecking order. To help stop bullying and fights it is usually better not to turn mares and geldings out together. Geldings may become territorial and start fights over mares, especially if there is a mare in season. Because of this many yards turn horses out in same sex groups.

Some people feel it is better not to turn a young horse out with older ones. If a group of young horses are turned out together they will amuse themselves, whereas a young horse with a group of older ones may either pester and annoy them or may well feel he has to fight to secure his status. Sometimes, however, a young strong-willed horse may be 'put in his place' by an older horse and disciplined into the pecking order.

A horse who is a bully can make life very difficult for an established group of horses. He will upset the status quo and keep 'pushing' until he is top of the pecking order. Once there he may continue bullying, particularly the horse who was previously top of the order.

Horses in stables

The best way to gain a horse's confidence in the stable is to be consistent in the way he is treated. Horses are creatures of habit and thrive when they have a regular routine.

Fair but firm handling is the way to ensure they are confident in their environment. Consistency in the behaviour of the handler will lead to consistency in the horse's behaviour.

Natural Horsemanship methods are becoming more popular with many horse owners. It should be remembered that these ideas tend to be based on generally accepted training methods of being consistent and confident around horses. Taking what happens within the herd in the wild and working to ensure that the handler becomes the 'herd' leader, the responses and timing the handler gives to the horse's behaviour form the basis of training. Many people who have an association with horses nowadays have not been brought up in a 'horsey' environment and so do not have that natural 'horse sense'. Natural Horsemanship methods can be one route to helping them understand how a horse learns and the effect their behaviour and responses can have on the horse.

Stable vices

The most common vices are weaving, crib-biting, wind-sucking and box walking.

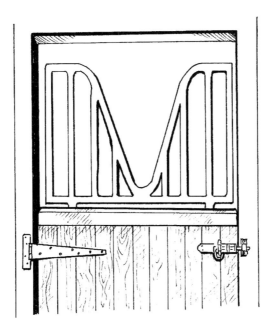

Stable door fitted with anti-weave bar

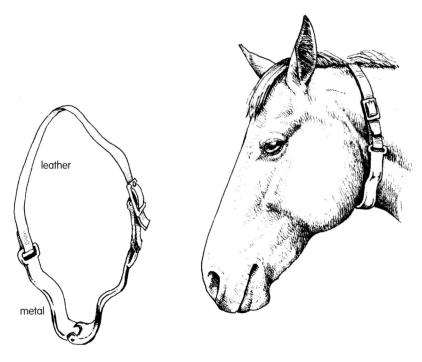

leather

metal

Anti-crib biting strap

Banging the stable door, kicking the stable walls and rug tearing are also bad repetitive habits.

Weaving is where the horse will stand with his head over the stable door and rock from side to side. This can lead to loss of condition and possible lameness in the front legs or feet, as the horse's weight is moved from side to side. Weaving can start when a horse in a stable sees other horses going out and he is left behind. It can also be caused by boredom, and some people feel that imitation of other horses may also be a factor. Anti-weaving bars on the stable door tend to alleviate this, although a confirmed weaver may stand behind the bars and weave. Turning the horse out as much as possible and ensuring ad lib bulk feed in his box may also help.

Crib-biting is when the horse takes hold of something (maybe the top of the stable door) and draws in air. Again it appears to be caused by boredom or imitation. Not having access to enough bulk food may also be a cause. Some people apply Cribox onto ledges within the stable which the horse could potentially take hold of. Others use a cribbing strap which makes it difficult for the horse to arch his neck when his teeth are holding a ledge. Turning the horse out may help, but some confirmed crib-biters will also find something to hold onto in the field.

Windsucking is a step further on from crib-biting. The horse will arch his neck and take in air. He no longer has a need to hold on to something to do this. As with crib-biting it can be caused by boredom, imitation and not enough bulk food. Turning out and a cribbing strap may help, but a confirmed wind-sucker can be very difficult to 'cure'.

If a horse with any of the three above is being sold then the vice must be declared to a potential purchaser.

Wood chewing is completely different to crib-biting. This is simply where the horse chews on any wooden parts of the stable, but does not grab the ledge and take in air. Many people mistake crib-biting for wood chewing.

Box walking is where the horse walks round and round in his box for long periods of time. A 'track' is left in the bedding of his box. It tends to be caused by boredom or even claustrophobia. A horse that is feeling ill may also box walk because of the pain. The horse may lose condition as he is not resting and there may well be a detrimental effect on the legs. Tuning out as much as possible and ad lib bulk food may help. If there is a possibility the horse is ill then the vet should be called.

Research into vices is ongoing. Keep up to date on the internet with theories and research conclusions.

It must be remembered that horses in the wild do not show these vices, so it is domestication that has caused them. We, as horse owners, are responsible by taking the horse out of his natural environment.

It appears to be the case that the more a horse is allowed freedom in a field with other horses the less likely vices are to appear. Regular work and being kept occupied with ad lib hay/haylage also seem to help.

Discomfort or undue stress in a horse's behaviour when he is ridden can be shown in many ways. Any alteration in his normal ridden behaviour should initially be taken as the possibility of pain or stress and not just put down to it being a 'bad day'. It must be remembered that a horse cannot verbally tell you if there is a problem, he can only do so by his behaviour. The following are some behaviour types that may show there is an issue:

- bucking

- rearing

- resistance in the mouth to the bit

- running away

- refusing to go forward or past something

- tightness in the back

- poor performance

- nervousness.

If any of these suddenly appear the rider needs to firstly find out if the horse is in any physical pain. This may be difficult as it could be one of a huge number of issues. It could be that the teeth need rasping or the horse has changed shape and the saddle is pinching. It may be that the horse has rolled in the field or in his box and has damaged his back. The possibilities go on and on and it may be necessary for the vet to be called to check the horse over.

    If no physical problem can be found then investigate the possibility of a mental one. Maybe he has been pushed too far too quickly in his work and feels nervous and insecure. Maybe he does not trust the rider or understand what is required. Once all physical and mental possibilities have been explored it may then be time to consider the fact that the horse is just being naughty and needs to be reprimanded. This route should, however, only be taken when the rider is 100% sure that there are no other issues.

What the assessor is looking for

- It is unlikely that there will be a horse in your exam who exhibits any stable vices and so almost certainly this information will be sought orally.

- You may be asked about horses living in a group situation (permanently at grass) and you should be able to talk about horses that may not be compatible with each other.

- There may be signs in the stable yard, such as anti-weaving bars, indicating that there are horses in the establishment that weave.

- Chewed wood in stables or on fences can also be a sign that horses have bad habits.

- You may be asked to discuss how you would know that a ridden horse was suffering discomfort or stress.

How to become competent

- You should ideally have seen a horse at some time who demonstrates these patterns of behaviour (but hopefully not one horse carrying out all these vices). If you have not seen all of them, then make sure that you have read about the habits you have not seen displayed and/or ask someone with more experience about them.

- Try to stay up to date with current thinking on this issue and ask your vet for his/her opinion.

- Any repetitive behaviour can have a detrimental effect on the horse's well-being and this should be recognised and understood.

- The more the vice is demonstrated then the more stress the horse is likely to be exhibiting.

- Make sure that you can describe the symptoms for all the vices that are listed above.

- Find out how the different vices might be 'treated', and talk to anyone who can give you first-hand information about dealing with behavioural traits.

- Rarely will horses demonstrate their vice when turned out at grass, although confirmed 'crib biters' will still find a fence to crib on. It is generally regarded as a remedy to turn the horse out as much as possible to give him plenty to occupy him and distract him from his bad habit.

- All behaviour traits demonstrated by the horse (particularly those he exhibits frequently rather than as a one-off reaction) tell you something about the personality of the horse.

- Make sure that you are able to recognise and relate to the nervous horse, the bossy horse, the horse with no manners, and the insecure horse. Learning to recognise a horse's 'personality' comes with practice – through looking after many horses and watching the way they relate to each other and to us.

- Remember that some behaviour patterns relate partly to the horse's natural instincts, while others are patterns that have developed as a learned response from what we do with the horse.

- Be aware of behavioural traits that might demonstrate discomfort or stress when the horse is being ridden.

- Take every opportunity to study a new horse coming into the yard. 'Read' every horse both in the stable and out, and learn to recognise the different traits demonstrated by each individual. This will enable you to become more aware and therefore better equipped to manage the horses in your care.

UNIT 4

Lunge a Fit Horse for Exercise

5 Credits

Lungeing

The candidate should be able to:

Lunge a fit horse for exercise.

Understand why and how horses are lunged.

To be competent for the lungeing section at Stage 3 the candidate must be more efficient and competent than at Stage 2 level. They are expected to be able to lunge a fit, experienced horse to ensure he is well exercised.

It is important when lungeing a horse for the candidate to show they are aware of his character and that a rapport is built up with him. Is he a backward-thinking horse that needs to be kept thinking forwards, or is he a sensitive horse that is easily upset, or something in between? At this level the candidate must be able to adapt their lungeing technique to suit the horse. Body language is vital when lungeing. The candidate must be positive but not domineering. A candidate who comes over as being shy and unsure of themselves will not gain the respect of the horse they are lungeing and invariably the horse will take charge. The voice should be positive, but not aggressive and there must be a difference between the tone used for upwards and downwards transitions. For an upwards transition the voice should be positive and encouraging, and for the downwards transitions the voice should be calmer and smoother. The aim should be for a harmonious communication between the candidate and the horse for the benefit of exercising him adequately.

Remember that the larger the circle the easier it is for the horse to work and keep his balance.

The handling of the equipment should be more effective and competent than at Stage 2 level. Check the tack before starting lungeing. The horse may be wearing a roller or a saddle. Check that the side-reins are approximately the length that will be required. To do this unclip the side-rein and hold it to the bit ring to give you an approximation. The candidate will be expected to use the side-reins when they feel the horse is ready.

Lunge the horse on both reins initially without the side-reins. If the candidate feels it would be beneficial to canter the horse then do so. A backward-thinking horse may well 'wake up' if cantered. When the horse is going forward adequately then attach the side-reins. They may not be at the length required. The candidate should show they have the experience and knowledge to quickly and efficiently adjust any design of side-rein to a desired length. If not practised at this the candidate can take up a considerable amount of the time allowed for this session and then will not have shown the assessor that they are competent at lungeing. If the candidate wishes to alter the length of the side-reins once the horse has been lunged in them for a few minutes then it is necessary to assess the horse and the situation to see if it is necessary to undo the side-reins to undertake this task. If the horse is showing he is not worried about what is going on and does not appear to be tense or anxious then, as long as the candidate is quick and efficient it may not be necessary to undo them. As a Stage 3 person the candidate should have the confidence and horse sense to judge this.

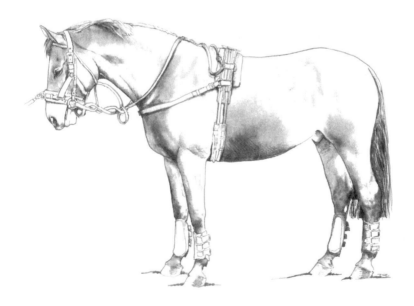

Horse tacked up for exercise on the lunge (without a rider)

Giving a lunge lesson. Rider working without stirrups in trot

Change the rein as frequently as necessary. It is not necessary to undo the side-reins when changing the rein as long as the horse and the situation have been assessed safely. The horse should be halted on the open part of the circle. The lunge line should be changed into the other hand before the candidate 'reels' themselves out to the horse. The horse should then be patted on the neck. The candidate should then walk round to the other side of the horse. The horse should then be sent away onto the other rein. By changing hands before the line is gathered up you are ensuring there will not be any twists when the line is let out again. By moving round the horse the candidate is not having to try and 'pull' the horse round with the side-reins attached. If the candidate feels that there may be a problem and the horse will be resistant then the side-reins should be undone, but this must be done quickly and efficiently.

At Stage 3 level the candidate should show exercises that will ensure the horse is lunged well for exercise. Frequent, well-produced transitions will help this, although a sharp horse may need a longer period of trot or canter to settle him first. Once the side-reins are attached then working to increase and decrease the size of the circle will help the horse to work harder. It will also help to show how established his rhythm and balance are. The candidate will need to take note of the horse's way of going. Is he rhythmical? If his balance is not good then he will not be able to keep a good rhythm. If he is stiff then he will not be able to balance himself and so will not show quality paces. Watch to see if he is tracking up in the trot and overtracking in walk. Does he swing through his back or is he tight? These issues should be mentioned in discussion with the assessor.

Also in discussion the candidate will be asked about the value of lungeing. Here are some of the many reasons why lungeing is valuable:

- It is an excellent way of starting to start work with a young horse.

- The horse can be worked harder in a shorter period of time than if being ridden.

- You can work a horse/pony you are too big to ride.

- A horse that may not be able to be ridden (e.g. a girth gall) can be exercised.

- It is something different to do as part of a training programme.

- The rider can see how the horse is moving and working.

- New movements can be taught – e.g. medium trot.

- A horse can be introduced to poles and jumps.

- Some people use lungeing to calm a fresh horse.

In discussion the candidate will also be asked to talk about the tack that has been used and the type of facilities that are required for safe lungeing.

This discussion is there for the candidate to show their depth of knowledge and experience. Look carefully at the equipment that has been used. Is the cavesson a good fit? Does the noseband droop down too low? Is it made of leather or webbing? Which do you prefer and why? How did the lunge line feel in the hand? Was it too thick, too thin, too slippery, too long, too short or did you feel comfortable using it? What were the side-reins like, and which type do you prefer, and why? What kind of attachment was there to fix the line to the cavesson? A Stage 3 candidate should have sensible opinions about all these items.

If the horse had a roller and you would prefer a saddle then you should give reasons why. How did the whip feel in your hand and was it long enough?

Three different types of side reins:

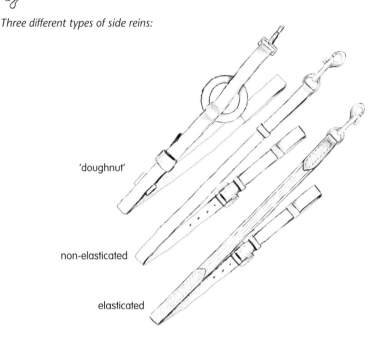

'doughnut'

non-elasticated

elasticated

The ideal facilities for lungeing are an enclosed outdoor or indoor school with a good non-slip surface. The perimeter fencing should be high enough to discourage the horse from thinking of jumping out and so that it can be used as a barrier by the person lungeing if necessary. If such an area is not available then a quiet corner in a flat field could be used. It would be useful to cordon off the area with poles and Bloks to then have four sides to work within. The going should not be too hard or too muddy so there is more possibility of the horse being able to keep his balance and not injure himself in any way.

What the assessor is looking for

- You were required to fit lunge equipment at Stage 2, so this knowledge should be secure. Now you should be able to glance at a horse equipped to lunge and be able to make any swift adjustment to ill-fitting or poorly applied tack.

- You will be expected to handle the lunge horse and the equipment provided competently and with familiarity. This enables you to demonstrate your ability to control an experienced fit horse, lungeing to exercise it to good effect. Your handling of the equipment must show a safe, secure lungeing technique.

- The exercises you choose should work the horse sufficiently, as if the session you are doing is the horse's only exercise for that day.

- You must show work that establishes the horse's rhythm and balance, with the horse going forward but without being hurried.

- You are likely to be asked about the value of lungeing – its worth to the horse, when you might use it, how long you might lunge for, and where you would choose to lunge the horse. Appropriate lungeing equipment is also likely to be discussed and may relate to the horse you have actually worked.

How to become competent

- There are no short-cuts to lungeing competence. Lungeing is an art like riding, and only practice and more practice will make you proficient.

- Even if you cannot lunge a horse very often, watch other people lungeing whenever you can.

- Practise the techniques for managing the lunge line and the whip (this does not have to be done with a horse). You can easily attach the end of the lunge line to a fence or ring; or ask a friend to hold the end of the rein while you practise paying the rein out, controlling the position of the whip, and gathering up the rein again, maintaining as level a contact on the rein as you can.

- When lungeing it is essential that you learn to put the horse out onto a contact on a circle of at least 15m, and preferably from 18m to 20m.

- Watch how more experienced people lunge and learn from them.

- The horse may be wearing a saddle or a roller, with a bridle and a lunge cavesson. It would be usual to have side-reins on the saddle in readiness for when the horse is going forward sufficiently. You should know that when lungeing a horse with a rider on top, the side-reins are purely to help keep the horse as straight as possible.

- Learn to use your voice in a positive and authoritative manner, in conjunction with your body language, to maintain control over the horse.

- Learn to maintain the horse's rhythm by developing a 'feel' for when to push the horse forward and when to 'hold hard' a little so as not to hassle the horse out of his natural rhythm.

- Be able to decrease and increase the size of the circle to work the horse further and encourage lateral suppleness. This, in conjunction with transitions from one pace to another, leads to activity, suppleness and obedience from the horse.

- Be able to make frequent transitions from one pace to another, as well as transitions within the pace, to encourage activity of the hind legs and obedience from the horse.

- In most cases, to lunge a horse to good effect it is usually necessary to work it in walk, trot and canter evenly on both reins. At this level you must feel confident to canter a horse on the lunge if you feel it would help him.

- In lungeing, as in riding, an important piece of advice is that you **must** have regular practice to develop the necessary feel and awareness.

STAGE 3
Riding Horses

IMPORTANT: Candidates are advised to check that they are working from the latest examination syllabus, as examination content and procedure are liable to alteration. Contact the BHS Examinations Office for up-to-date information regarding the syllabus.

Syllabus

Candidates should show a feel for their horses and have an appreciation of any weakness. They should begin to school the horses and to ride them according to their needs.

Candidates who are considered to be below the standard will be asked to retire.

About the riding examination

By the time you reach this level, your basic riding position should be established and secure and you should be seeking to develop greater depth and effectiveness through the regular daily riding of as many different horses as possible.

Working without stirrups on a regular basis will help to deepen your seat and develop suppleness, greater feel and co-ordination of the aids. You must fully understand the aids you are using to create forward movement through the horse's basic gaits. You must be able to have a positive influence on the horses that you ride, being able to maintain their level of work and show an ability to ride them effectively between the leg and hand, if their level of training and cooperation allows this.

In the section devoted to riding horses on the flat, you will ride two horses, and on at least one of these must show an ability to ride competently without your stirrups in all three basic gaits. On both horses you should demonstrate an ability to find rhythm and harmony with the horse in a relatively short period of time, showing some ability to adapt to find the effect that achieves the feel for that horse. The horses should be sufficiently educated that they will work into a round connection between hand and leg in snaffle bridles. They should be able to work through the basic gaits, through loops, serpentines and circles and show simple exercises such as turn about the forehand, leg yielding and shortening and lengthening of stride in all three paces. You must be able to relate to the strengths and weaknesses in the horses you ride, both in your practical demonstration of riding ability and in discussion.

The riding at Stage 3 level should demonstrate an evolving competence and confidence in your own ability and the basic initiative to be in control of all situations on trained horses, which may have the ability and enthusiasm to show a little more individuality and need for authority from the rider than the horses presented for riding at Stage 2.

If you are unsuccessful in the flatwork riding you will not be able to go forward to the jumping section. If you are unsuccessful in the show jumping section you will not be allowed to ride cross-country. This rule has been introduced not only for the safety of riders and horse but also for the welfare of the horses. The rider can be stopped at any stage of the flat and jumping section. It is vital that candidates are confident to ride and jump unknown horses to this level.

FLAT
Ride Horses on the Flat
26 credits / 169 guided learning hours

Unit Purpose and Aims
The learner will be able to ride and work horses to 'Novice Dressage' level, showing a secure, supple, independent and balanced position. They will have a degree of 'feel' that recognises the level of the horse's way of going. They will be able to utilise a plan of work including transitions and exercises to maintain the horse's way of going. They will build up a rapport and show respect for the horse being ridden. The learner will also understand how to evaluate and progress the horse's work. The Learner will be able to work safely and efficiently with minimum supervision and will exhibit the autonomy required by the industry for career progression to a more senior post or in order to develop further skills, knowledge and understanding necessary for a Level 4 qualification.

Learner Outcomes		Assessment Criteria	
The Learner will		The Learner can	
1.	Be able to ride and work horses effectively in walk, trot and canter, with and without stirrups	1.1	Walk, trot and canter maintaining a balanced, independent and supple seat, with and without stirrups
		1.2	Ride the horses forward into a receiving hand
		1.3	Use fluent and co-ordinated natural and artificial aids to prepare for and ride transitions and exercises including moving away from the leg to maintain the horses quality of work
		1.4	Ride to a appropriate plan of work for the horse being ridden
2.	Be able to ride and work horses independently within a group	2.1	Abide by the rules of the school when riding with others in open order
		2.2	Show consideration for and awareness of others when riding
3.	Be able to ride and work horses sympathetically	3.1	Respect the horse and build up a rapport when riding
		3.2	Ride and work in harmony with the horse
		3.3	Ride and work the horse within its capabilities
4.	Know and understand the training of the horse to 'Novice Dressage' level	4.1	Explain the basic principles of training horses
		4.2	Draw conclusions about the ridden horse's way of going
		4.3	Suggest suitable exercises for the continuation of the horse's work

JUMPING
Ride Horses over Fences
26 credits / 169 guided learning hours

Unit Purpose and Aims
The learner will be able to prepare for and ride horses over a course of show jumps up to 1m/3'3" and a cross-country course up to 90cm in a confident, secure, balanced and independent position, with due consideration for the horse's welfare. The learner will also understand how to evaluate and progress the horse's work. The Learner will be able to work safely and efficiently with minimum supervision and will exhibit the autonomy required by the industry for career progression to a more senior post or in order to develop further skills, knowledge and understanding necessary for a Level 4 qualification.

Learner Outcomes	Assessment Criteria	
The Learner will	The Learner can	
1. Be able to walk show jumping and cross country courses	1.1	Walk a route suitable for riding a show jump course and a cross country course giving due consideration to the state of going and external influences.
2. Be able to ride in preparation for jumping including a grid of fences	2.1	Ride with confidence in a secure, balanced and independent position with due consideration for the horse's welfare.
	2.2	Carry out suitable warm-up exercises for jumping taking ground, weather conditions and other riders into account
	2.3	Ride correct approaches to the grid
	2.4	Ride with rhythm and balance
3. Be able to ride over a course of show jumps (up to 1m/3'3")	3.1	Ride with confidence in a secure, balanced and independent position with due consideration for the horse's welfare.
	3.2	Ride correct approaches to fences
	3.3	Ride with rhythm and balance
4. Be able to ride over a cross-country course (up to 0.9m/3')	4.1	Ride with confidence in a secure, balanced and independent position with due consideration for the horse's welfare
	4.2	Carry out suitable warm-up exercises for riding cross-country taking ground, weather conditions and other riders into account
	4.3	Ride with pace, rhythm and balance
	4.4	Ride correct approaches to fences
5. Understand how to evaluate and progress a horse's work	5.1	Describe the ridden horse's way of going
	5.2	Evaluate it's performance
	5.3	Suggest suitable exercises for the continuation of the horse's work

In the jumping section you will again ride two horses: one over show jumps and one over cross-country fences. You must demonstrate confidence and competence to ride with security and effect over a small course of fences on trained horses. In the show-jumping work, the jumping will develop over a progressive grid of fences and will culminate in jumping a numbered course (see above for suggested course plans). In the cross-country section you will ride a second horse over a short course of straightforward schooling-type fixed obstacles, where you should demonstrate a pace appropriate to cross-country riding while taking into account the ground conditions.

UNIT 1
Ride Horses on the Flat

26 Credits

The candidate should be able to:

Ride and work horses effectively in walk, trot and canter with or without stirrups.

What the assessor is looking for

- You may be asked to give a leg-up to another candidate, probably when you change horses after your first ride.

- Make sure you put your whip down. Bear in mind that you will probably not know the person you are legging up so the instructions between you must be clear. Often a poor leg-up occurs because the two people involved are not co-ordinated and one pushes when the other is not ready. If you are used to giving or receiving a leg-up on a count of three, then it is essential that only one person does the counting! If you both count together you can be sure that one of you will be out of sync. Suggest to the person receiving the leg-up that he counts and you will push on 'three'. Similarly when you are being given the leg-up, tell the person throwing you up that you will count and they are to push as you count 'three' because that is when you will spring.

- The whole essence of a leg-up is that the rider is given an additional boost to his spring, to put him up onto the horse. Thus the 'spring' is essential.

- The ability to give and receive a leg-up is important at this level because there may be instances (such as dealing with a young horse or remounting a rider with short stirrups) when this is the most practical and efficient way of remounting a rider.

- You must demonstrate a practical competence to both give and receive a leg-up to a standard which would be safe in any given situation. It must not end up as a struggle with the rider clambering onto the horse's back.

- The following require that you demonstrate your basic position and security at this level, and from that basic position the ability to ride horses forward, influencing them with clear and consistent aids.

- Your position should be well established, with good balance and poise. Your balance should stem from sitting evenly in the saddle with the weight over both seat bones; an imaginary line from your ear, through the shoulder, the hip and

Correct basic riding position

into the heel, and another, running from the elbow through the wrist to the horse's mouth, should be clear.

- This balance and consistency in position should be maintained as you absorb and follow the horse's movement, thus demonstrating suppleness and an awareness of how the horse is moving under you.

- As a result of a secure position and a clear understanding of aid application you should be able to ride the horses forward to a receiving hand. At this level your position must be sufficiently deep and balanced for your aids to be applied with clarity, independence and effect.

- This section is the underpinning foundation for the whole of your riding and as such is vitally important at this level. Do not underestimate the standard required.

- You will be expected to demonstrate your basic balance, suppleness and effect in all three paces on the horses you ride.

151

- In the exam (as at any time) your work without stirrups should deepen and relax you, making you more at one with the horse and allowing you to develop your partnership with the horse more effectively.

How to become competent

- In your training you should be riding without stirrups almost every day or at least every time you ride on the flat.

- It cannot be stressed too highly that riding without stirrups consistently improves your depth and security probably more effectively than any other form of work.

- Be passionate about your position. Be determined to improve it and develop it to be deeper, more supple, more co-ordinated and more effective every time you ride.

- You cannot ride enough different horses – they can all teach you something a little different. Learn to 'read' them before you get on and 'feel' them once you are riding.

- Work on your poise and balance as well as your effectiveness.

- Consider the aids you are trying to give and constantly be aware of the response that each horse gives you.

Horse and rider in balance and harmony. Horse working in a soft, round form accepting the rider's aids

Loss of harmony. Horse showing resistance and hollowness; rider showing tension and stiffness in position

Horse dropping behind the contact, overbent with nose behind the vertical and poll too low

- Be aware of the importance of good preparation and consistency in the aids that you are using.

- When a horse apparently does not respond, think through your preparation and the aids you gave, consider your effect and whether reinforcement via the whip is appropriate.

- Learn to experiment; find out what works and what causes resistance and loss of harmony; learn to be effective; some horses need very positive aids, others need a much lighter approach.

- All horses need consistent information, which they must have from consistent thinking and aid application from you.

- Make quite sure that you understand what 'forward' really means. Forward is activity with rhythm and balance and harmony; forward is not running along out of balance, associated with tension and lack of suppleness in the horse.

- Practise giving and receiving a leg-up. Watch those who work in the racing industry to see a leg-up given well. It depends on co-ordination between the person giving the leg-up and rider. It has nothing to do with the strength of the person on the ground and everything to do with lightness, spring and co-ordination between the two involved.

- If you have to count to give a leg up, make quite sure that the timing between you is immaculate and the rider does 'spring'.

- This section needs a fundamental consistency and must be very established and secure at this level. It is the mainstay of much of the rest of the work to be demonstrated as a Stage 3 rider.

The candidate should be able to:

Ride and work independently within a group.

What the assessor is looking for

- You will ride two horses in an approximately 50-minute period and there will be up to five of you riding at the same time. The work is directed only generally, in that you will be asked to work to establish a good rhythm and balance in all three gaits. It is then up to you to choose work that is appropriate to the horse you are riding while working the horse in walk, trot and canter in your own time.

- You must demonstrate a clear programme of work that is appropriate for developing rhythm and suppleness.

- You should therefore be showing some large circles, loops and serpentines all of which are clear in what they are meant to be (size and shape).

- You should demonstrate clear preparation for all your work, showing smooth transitions from one pace to another and also within the paces (shortening and lengthening the trot and canter, and not forgetting the walk).

- At any time the assessor should be able to look at you and recognise what you are trying to do and what figure you might be riding.

- Everything about your riding should look well prepared and planned, and nothing should look hurried or hastily decided.

- You should always look as if you are riding in your own designated space with no one around you. This indicates a clear awareness of other riders and where they are going, while you are always planning to stay in a space to give your horse the best possible area in which to work.

- There is no harm in giving a horse a short, sharp reminder with a schooling whip if he constantly ignores your aid – in fact, the assessor would prefer to see you using judgement according to the way the horse is going.

- It is essential that you feel what is going on under you and 'read' the situation so that your response and choice of how best to influence the horse is well considered and effective.

How to become competent

- Confidence in your own ability is absolutely essential. (The assessors do not want to see arrogance, but confidence based on competence and self-belief.)

- You cannot ride too many horses to teach you and upgrade your awareness and effect.

- Training is vital, but try not to learn only during your training sessions or you can become over-dependent on your instructor and rely on him giving you the competence and taking responsibility for 'getting it right'.

- Try to ride 'out and about' as well as in the school. This will teach you to act on your own initiative and find out what works and what doesn't. If you are being run away with in a wide-open space you soon learn to 'take control'! Similarly, if you are out in the countryside and your friends have all jumped a small ditch and your horse is lacking a bit of courage, you will soon learn to 'kick and hold the mane', or encourage him in some other way to be a bit braver and go on. You will learn from these experiences and be a better rider for them.

- Make sure that you are quite clear on the 'floor plan' of the regular school movements used on a daily basis. Circles of 20m, 15m and 10m should all be recognisable, as should 5m loops, three- and four-loop serpentines, turns across the school, and use of the short and long diagonals.

- Maintaining the horse 'in good form' relates to your ability to show the horse working in a good rhythm (regularity) in all three gaits. Also evident should be a consistent connection between the leg and hand and harmony between you and the horse. The horse should show a bend in the direction in which he is going, and you should constantly be able to demonstrate a desire to achieve some suppleness through turns, corners and circles even on the 'stiff side'.

The candidate should be able to:

Ride and work horses sympathetically.

What the assessor is looking for

- All the work in this section continue to demonstrate your competence at this level.

- All the work you show – transitions and school figures – should show clear preparation and execution.

- You will be given minimal direction as to what to do in your riding of the horses, but your competence at this level should enable you to choose work that will increase the horse's obedience and suppleness.

- You should show an awareness of work that is satisfactory by rewarding the horse (pat on the neck) after some work you are pleased with, and move on as a result of the satisfactory work to something more demanding. (For example, if 20m circles are good then move on to 15m and then to 10m; or if a turn about the forehand is good, move on to leg-yield.)

- Similarly, if during a turn about the forehand the horse is resistant or walks out half way through, show an awareness by going back to try to improve the result.

- Planning is essential and should be evident. (For example, starting with a 10m circle when the horse is not forward or supple would demonstrate a lack of awareness and planning. Likewise, starting in canter before the horse is settled and rhythmical in walk and trot is probably unwise.)

- The work should show a smooth progression through circles, turns and transitions, using turns about the forehand to see if the horse understands about moving away from the leg. Make a clear demonstration of understanding how to ride a turn on the forehand (from halt) and a turn about the forehand (from walk). In both cases show the correct position, staying over the centre of the horse and apply clear and co-ordinated aids (slight flexion, inside leg behind the girth to move the hindquarters around, outside leg keeping the horse forward and stopping him from trying to step backwards, outside rein preventing the horse from moving forwards and controlling the degree of neck bend). (*Note: Always, 'inside' refers to the way in which the horse is bending – e.g. if bent to the right, the inside leg and inside rein are the right rein and leg.*)

- Once you have discovered how the horse responds to your leg by riding some turns about the forehand then progressing to some leg-yielding would be appropriate. You must demonstrate an awareness of the movement by keeping the horse straight (apart from very slight flexion away from the direction of movement) and then moving the horse forwards and sideways away from your inside leg. The horse's inside hind leg should step more under his body to carry him forwards and sideways without him falling out through the outside shoulder. Co-ordination of your aids is essential here, with your outside leg keeping the horse forward while your inside leg moves the horse sideways; the inside rein maintains the flexion while the outside rein regulates the pace and controls the amount of flexion in the neck. Rhythm is always still a priority.

- Rein-back may also be requested, with you showing a feel for asking the horse to move backwards from a balanced halt. A feel for riding two or three steps and then moving forward again, rewarding the horse, is important. You should show an awareness of when the horse is able to move back with a supple back, in a submissive connection between leg and hand, and when he is hollow in the back and inclined to resist the aids.

How to become competent

- Much of what has already been said in the riding section applies here.

- There is no substitute for riding as many different horses as possible to develop your feel and awareness of the way in which horses respond to your aids.

- Make sure that you receive plenty of sound instruction on how to ride the developing work; be aware of turn about the forehand, leg-yielding and rein-back in terms of complete understanding of what the movements are, how the horse moves through them and what aids you should be using to effect the correct response.

- Ride these movements often within your pattern of work so that they become very familiar to you and you do not have to think what aids you are using – they come automatically. Once you are not having to think the aids through then you can begin to concentrate more on the preparation and feeling of what is happening underneath you.

- Watch videos of horses performing movements correctly so that you are familiar with what they look like when carried out well. Sit in with a dressage judge, if you have the chance, so that you can watch riders riding movements and listen to the comments made about the quality of the movements. This will also give you an insight into the way a rider prepares for the exercise and the quality of the work that is being presented.

The candidate should be able to:

Know and understand the training of the horse to 'Novice Dressage' level.

What the assessor is looking for

- At the end of riding either one or both horses you will be asked about the horse and what you have found out about his way of going.

- What you say about the horse must show clearly that you understand how a horse should be trained and the basic principles of training.

- Your comments about the horse should reflect your ability to assess the rhythm, suppleness and forwardness of the horse.

- You should be able to recognise whether or not the horse worked from activity in the hind legs, over a supple back and neck, into a submissive connection in the rein.

- From rhythm, suppleness and connection, you would be able to assess how straight the horse is and how much energy is forthcoming.

- Talk about whether or not the horse has a stiffer side, and a soft or hollow side. This relates to the horse's ease of bending on one rein and more reluctance to bend on the other rein.

- On the soft side it is necessary to limit the natural desire of the horse to bend only through his neck and then fall out through the outside shoulder, thus avoiding the energy coming through a 'straight' body to the rein.

- On the stiff side, where the horse is reluctant to bend and maintain activity with the inside hind leg stepping sufficiently under his body, there is then a tendency for him to tip his head to the outside, so avoiding the bend.

- Be able to talk systematically about the horse – avoid jumping from one trait to another.

- Every horse has something in his favour, so get into the habit of bringing out the positive before discussing the negative aspects of the work. For example: 'The horse was quite amenable and obedient, but was a little stiff to the left and reluctant to really go forward from my leg aids,' sounds very different to: 'The horse was stiff and lazy and I didn't like him.'

- Your comments about the horse(s) must apply to the horse(s) that you have actually ridden; they should not be just a stereotyped description which could apply to any horse.

How to become competent

- There are many good books available on training horses; read as much as you can to consolidate your theoretical knowledge.

- Sit in with a dressage judge so that you can watch horses working at Novice and Elementary level to help you understand the quality of good movement and become familiar with terms such as rhythm, suppleness, submission and impulsion and where they apply to the horse's way of going.

- Make sure that you discuss with your instructor the way of going of the horses you ride so that you develop greater understanding of what the horse is doing underneath you.

- Practise talking about horses that you ride so that you are familiar with assessing them in a practical, systematic way.

UNIT 2
Ride Horses over Fences

26 Credits

The candidate should be able to:

Prepare and ride horses over a course of show jumps up to 1m (3' 3") and a cross-country course up to 90 cm (3') in a confident, secure, balanced and independent position with due consideration for the horse's welfare.

What the assessor is looking for

- In the jumping unit you will ride two horses: one over show jumps and the other over cross-country fences.

- You must be able to walk both courses being able to work out distances between fences and how the state of going and external influences might affect your work.

- In the jumping unit of the exam you will be required to show a secure and balanced position which will sustain you to ride the horse in harmony over undulating ground and around show jumps and cross-country fences.

- The show jumping may be on grass or it may be on an artificial surface. The cross-country jumping will, of course, be on grass. In every situation you must be able to judge the ground underneath you and choose the gait and speed according to the 'going'. This will ensure a balanced ride.

- In the cross-country phase you should be able to show an increased pace appropriate to cross-country riding, if the ground conditions allow it.

- The show jumping will be built up progressively through a grid of fences, and then you will be required to jump a course of show jumps at approximately 1m height (3ft 3in).

- Across country you will be required to jump a course of five to ten straightforward fixed obstacles, which may involve some variations in gradient and terrain.

- Throughout this section your balance and harmony with the horse must be consistent, emanating from a well-established confident jumping position.

- You must demonstrate confidence, independence and initiative in your jumping ability.

How to become competent

- Always walk your couses before riding them.

- Take every opportunity to attend organised course walks.

- Walk courses with as many knowledgeable people as you can.

- Learn to stride distances accurately.

- Jump, jump and jump some more! There is no substitute for practice.

- Just as with your position for riding on the flat, your jumping position needs much practice to consolidate your balance, security and confidence.

- Ride lots of horses that jump genuinely – maintaining a good rhythm and balance to a fence and then jumping fluently when they get there.

- Jump gymnastic exercises without your stirrups to develop feel and balance and improve your security and effect.

- If you are able to do any competitive jumping then this is useful.

- Clear-round jumping at a local competition and perhaps some cross-country schooling, will all help you to develop an independence in your jumping.

The candidate should be able to:

Ride in preparation for jumping including a grid of fences.

What the assessor is looking for

- The foundation for jumping well, in balance and harmony with the horse, is a good basic jumping position.

- The jumping position depends on balance, and the security of a jumping position comes from the lower leg. If the lower leg slips forward, the rider's upper body may tip back out of balance; and if the rider's lower leg slips back; the upper body may tip forward and the balance will be lost.

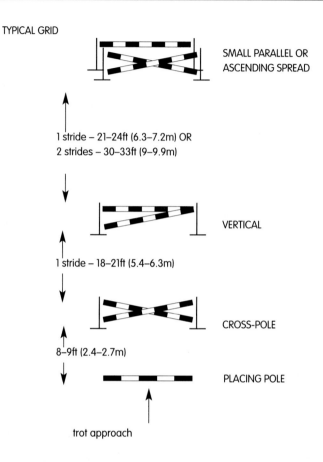

TYPICAL GRID

SMALL PARALLEL OR
ASCENDING SPREAD

1 stride – 21–24ft (6.3–7.2m) OR
2 strides – 30–33ft (9–9.9m)

VERTICAL

1 stride – 18–21ft (5.4–6.3m)

CROSS-POLE

8–9ft (2.4–2.7m)

PLACING POLE

trot approach

- The grid will be built up from a cross-pole, probably with a placing pole from a trot approach. After jumping this once or twice, a second fence will be introduced at one non-jumping stride distance from the first. The approach will still be from trot.

- On each occasion it is important that you ride a well-planned line of approach with a straight line to the centre of the first fence, maintaining rhythm and impulsion in the approach.

- As the grid develops you will be invited to jump it several times until you are comfortable with the rhythm and pace for your approach.

- A third fence will be built either one or two non-jumping strides from the second fence, and again the initial approach will still be made in trot unless you have a short striding horse.

- Throughout the grid work you should show a fluency in your jumping position, with your balance and security of position allowing you to maintain an allowing hand to the horse over the fences.

- The warm-up for both the show jumping and cross-country should demonstrate your ability to prepare the horse to jump.

- You should be working in at jumping length and in jumping position (light seat/half seat/poised position).

- Your work should involve transitions, shortening and lengthening (particularly in canter), and perhaps some direct transitions (halt to trot and walk to canter) to demonstrate that the horse is actively in front of your leg.

- Your work should involve an awareness of ground conditions. If the ground is slippery then you should show judgement of pace, particularly around corners, not making any turns too acute.

- Similarly if it is a cold day and the horse is clipped and feeling a bit full of himself, you should move him around actively to warm him up as soon as possible; whereas on a hot muggy day you may give the horse a break to avoid overstressing him.

- You may be asked about your warm up and you should be able to talk about the preparation in terms of wanting the horse to be warmed up through his muscles, obedient and listening to the aids and in control.

- After any of your jumping sessions you should be sure to allow the horse to get his breath back (especially after cross-country) by walking him around.

- You should also show an awareness of the need to allow the horse to relax, perhaps loosening the girth and dismounting if appropriate.

- In discussion you should be aware of the need to allow a horse to cool down gradually, throwing a sheet over his loins and back, particularly if a cold day, to prevent him from catching a chill.

- You may be asked about when and whether you would wash a horse off after competition and how you would look after him following exertion.

How to become competent

- No apology is made for repeating the word practice again and again, because there is no substitute for practice. It is the only way that you will ultimately achieve competence.

- As much grid work as possible will help you to develop a feel for the horse's stride and balance.

- Learn to feel how varying the energy in the approach can affect the feel through the grid.

- When distances are measured exactly between fences to produce a specific number of strides (in this case one and then two) there can be some difference in the feel of fluency over those fences, depending on the speed or energy in the approach.

- If the horse rushes into the placing pole, hurrying over it and bounding into canter, the first distance (which is measured to be taken from a calm trot approach) will feel short and tight.

- If the horse then continues to rush, the next distance will also feel short and tense.

- It is important that you learn to feel the speed of the pace of approach and be able to adapt it if necessary. If the horse is lazy and inactive then you must be able to influence it for greater energy and activity.

- Similarly if the horse is hurried and rushing then a slower pace in the approach or a shorter approach may help to address the problem.

- Some jumping work down a controlled grid without your stirrups, on an obedient horse that you have jumped several times before, will help develop your security and independence.

- Some jumping work down a controlled grid without your reins (knot them on the neck for easy access, if required), on an obedient horse that you have jumped several times before, will help to develop your feel, fluency and independence.

- The warm-up for jumping is vital to the success of the jumping session.

- If the horse is not sufficiently warmed up, loosened up and on the aids then he is more likely to knock show jumps down, run out or refuse both show jumps and cross-country fences.

- Learn to warm up effectively feeling the horse's responsiveness and suppleness, and then learn to use fences progressively, building up in difficulty to develop the horse's confidence and commitment.

- Be able to shorten and lengthen the stride particularly in canter and with regard to cross-country, open the horse up with a short, sharp strong canter or half-speed gallop over a bigger straight distance (50–100 metres/yards).

- Always find out from the horse you are riding, how much 'instant' acceleration he will give you and then how effectively he will come back to you when you ask him to slow down.

- Discuss with anyone you know who competes in eventing how they warm up for show jumping and cross-country and what they do when they have completed those phases.

- Read books about training for competitions, particularly eventing (which covers a show jumping and cross-country phase).

The candidate should be able to:

Ride over a couse of show jumps (up to 1m/3' 3").

Understand how to evaluate and progress a horse's work.

What the assessor is looking for

- Having showed progressive work building up over a grid of three fences you will then be required to jump a course of fences which will include a double (of one or two non-jumping strides).

- You will ride the same horse that you have ridden through the grid work, and the grid should act as a good warm-up so that by now you have developed a rapport with the horse and a feel for how he jumps.

- Once you have warmed the horse up you may be asked about his way of going and how you feel he will jump the course.

- One at a time, and usually in numerical order, you will jump the course of show jumps, which you should have walked on arrival at the exam centre.

- In jumping the course you must ride a good track, planning your corners and lines of approach and departure to and from each fence.

- Throughout the course you must sustain a good balanced position, going fluently with the horse and allowing him freedom over the fences.

- The pace you choose should be appropriate to the horse, the ground conditions and the jumps you are trying to negotiate.

- You might bring the horse back to trot to ride a tight corner if you are on grass and the ground is slippery.

- You would lack judgement of the correct pace if you chose to approach a double of one non-jumping stride (with a distance of 24ft/7.8m) from trot, as the horse would then probably struggle to make the one stride.

- In jumping the course you must show a positive and effective manner, which comes from confidence and competence at this level.

- You must also be able to deal with minor problems which might arise within the course. If the horse refuses or runs out at a jump, this in itself is not necessarily your fault, but the way in which you deal with the problem will reflect your competence.

- You will need to describe the horse's way of going and evaluate its performance. This should then be linked to exercises that could be used to improve his show jumping technique.

How to become competent

- With regard to the security of your jumping position refer back to earlier advice on improving your position and effect.

- You can only sustain your jumping position and develop its effect and your confidence and competence by plenty of repetition.

- Jumping occasionally, or even once a week, will not convey the competence and therefore confidence that comes from jumping frequently and on several different horses.

- It is possible to improve your jumping position, balance and security by working on the flat in jumping position. Varying your position from sitting to rising, and also standing up in your stirrups so that you learn to find your point of balance over your lower leg, will help strengthen your position. This work should be done in trot and canter so that your jumping position is both flexible and versatile.

- In addition to jumping grids where distances are measured for you and so you know where the horse will take off for each fence, you must also jump plain fences, and courses of fences where you have to link jumps together.

- The fluency of a course is dependent on you being able to maintain the pace through corners and lines of approach, and also in departures, where the horse may lose rhythm as a result of the jump.

- You must learn to judge pace and show the difference between balanced, controlled energy and uncontrolled speed.

- Rhythm and control of pace will enable the horse to jump in a fluent harmonious way, which you should find easier to follow and stay in balance with.

- If the horse is awkward or disobedient and either runs out or refuses at a fence, you must have enough confidence to make a decision about how to correct the horse.

- Learning to make corrections with horses who are awkward about jumping comes from confidence of riding horses who need encouragement or firmness to develop their jumping.

- A well-timed smack with the whip to correct a horse who has been disobedient can be acceptable, but the whip use must be immediately relevant to the fault (e.g. immediately after a refusal and while the horse is still in front of the fence).

- Untimely use of the whip and use of the whip on the neck is rarely helpful in effecting a positive outcome to a fault.

- The more secure your position, and the more horses you have jumped, the more confident you will be in ensuring that any horse goes over a fence if you have directed him at it.

- Confidence develops competence and vice versa.

- Go to jumping competitions and watch how other riders negotiate courses.

- Attend training days and schooling sessions.

- Read show jumping training books.

- Walk courses so that you are familiar with the way courses develop in difficulty and how corners and changes of rein are built into jumping courses.

- Look at the way jumps are built with fillers to back the horse off or make the jump look more imposing, narrow jumps (stiles) which need more accuracy in riding, and vertical and oxer-type fences.

- If at all possible do some competing yourself, as this always conveys a flair, determination and initiative in your riding that is difficult to achieve from any other source.

- Clear-round jumping at a local venue, Riding Club competitions, unaffiliated classes and then affiliated BSJA classes will all offer something for the developing jumping rider.

The candidate should be able to:

Ride over a cross-country course (up to 0.9m/3').

Understand how to evaluate and progress a horse's work.

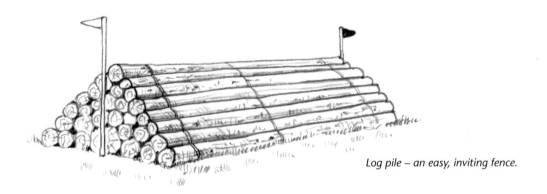

Log pile – an easy, inviting fence.

Raised log – a solid fence but with no clear groundline, making it a little more difficult for the horse to judge the point of take-off.

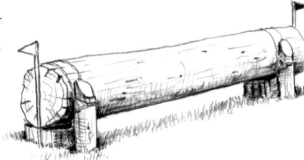

What the assessor is looking for

- As with the show-jumping phase, the examiner is looking for a purposeful, confident approach so that you ride the horse competently round a simple course of fences.

- You will have changed horses from your show-jumping ride, but you must still show a secure and balanced position in harmony with the horse. The security of your position must allow you to ride the horse with influence and control, producing a fluent round with an allowing hand over the fences.

- You must show an understanding of a pace appropriate to cross-country riding, but this will be relevant to the ground conditions (e.g. if the ground is very slippery or hard you might adjust the pace to a slower speed, particularly around corners or turns). It is also important to ride the horse in a good rhythm.

- The terrain and fence type should also influence your choice of pace (e.g. if jumping down steps or a drop fence, you will need to reduce the pace – while maintaining the power – so that the horse can jump off his hocks and not tip onto the forehand as he lands). You might choose a strong trot or a contained canter rather than a 'forward' canter.

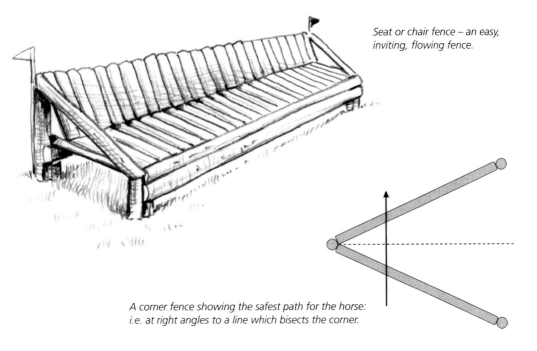

Seat or chair fence – an easy, inviting, flowing fence.

A corner fence showing the safest path for the horse: i.e. at right angles to a line which bisects the corner.

- You must show an awareness of how to choose an appropriate approach for a variety of fence types. Here you should be aware that for angled fences or corners you may still need to choose a straight line at right angles to the fence to allow the horse to jump it with maximum ease.

- You must show some ability to deal with refusals or run-outs in much the same way as was referred to in the previous element.

- You may be asked about the horse's way of going and to evaluate his performance. You may then be asked to suggest suitable exercises to improve his cross-country technique.

How to become competent

- Much of the advice given in the preceding element on show jumping applies here, but with specific reference to cross-country riding.

- Try to attend some good events (British Eventing affiliated competitions) and watch cross-country riding. Especially watch the professional riders and see the fluency and rhythm with which they jump their courses.

- The better the rhythm, the easier it is for the horse to negotiate the jumps.

- Learn to jump cross-country fences from a much stronger canter than you would use for a standard show-jumping round.

- Learn to ride canter easily up and down hills, feeling the balance of the horse and allowing him to use himself up and down gradients.

- Continually consolidate your own balance and position by riding in jumping position frequently (not just when you are jumping).

- Your jumping position will only become really secure and established with much practice.

- Try to take any opportunity to ride cross-country fences, whether in a schooling session, on a cross-country ride with some jumps, or at a one-day event.

- Attend training days and schooling sessions.

- Read cross-country training books.

STAGE 3
Questions and Answers

Below are some of the suggested questions/tasks relating to the Stage 3 syllabus. Some questions are accompanied by a concise, model answer (or answers) indicating an acceptable level of knowledge; others give advice on how to approach answering them. In every case you should try to enhance your answer to show a greater depth of knowledge. A more expansive answer requires that you study each subject a little more deeply, which will enable you to speak with greater confidence when giving your answers.

Structure of the leg below the knee

Q. Using the horse in front of you, show me where you might expect to find a splint.

A. Be able to designate the area where a splint might be present, which is in the region below the knee and anywhere to approximately half way down the cannon bone towards the back of the limb where the splint bones lie.

Splints can be present on the front or hind legs; they may be on the inside or outside of the limb, although they are more commonly found on the inside of the front limb.

Q. What could be a possible cause of the horse developing splints, and how are they normally treated?

A. The development of a splint(s) is usually associated with working young horses excessively on hard ground or too much work for the horse whose bone development is still youthful and potentially vulnerable to jarring or over-work.

Splints do, however, occasionally arise through no fault of the horse owner or rider, and can do so in older horses.

Generally the treatment should involve taking the horse out of work, especially while the splint is in the developing stage. The horse may be slightly lame, and the splint may be hot and show some inflammation as it establishes.

Cold hosing will alleviate some heat and discomfort.

Usually splints cause little problem as long as they are not aggravated by hard work during development.

Q. Using the horse in front of you, name the main tendons in the lower leg and show me where they run on the horse.

A. Here you must demonstrate confidence and be able to show directly on the limb where the following tendons run:

- Common digital extensor tendon (front of limb).

- Lateral digital extensor tendon (front of limb).

- Superficial digital flexor tendon (back of limb).

- Deep digital flexor tendon (back of limb).

Q. If a horse strains a tendon what are the likely signs and how is it treated? Can we ever tell if a horse has strained a tendon in the past?

A. The horse is likely to go suddenly lame, or after a hard day's exertion the lower limb (in the tendon region) is likely to swell, show heat and pain on pressure.

The horse should be rested immediately; the vet should be called, as an assessment must be made and the horse may need some pain relief.

Cold hosing is likely to help in relieving the pain, heat and swelling.

The vet should advise on the immediate and longer-term treatment.

Generally, tendon injuries need time for healing.

A limb that has suffered a tendon injury is likely to show some residual damage:

> (a) The limb should be cold, but there may be thickening in the tendon region where some rupturing of the tendon sheath or fibres caused scar tissue to develop in the repair of the injury.

> (b) The tendon may look 'bowed'.

Q. Show me on the horse in front of you where you would expect to find windgalls. Has the horse got any? Do they need to be treated, and, if so, how?

A. Be sure to know where windgalls occur (small, puffy soft lumps around the fetlock joint, usually on both front or both hind legs – windgalls on a single leg may be a sign of a more serious problem in the affected leg).

Be sure that you can recognise windgalls when they are present.

Usually windgalls do not cause a problem. They are, however, an indication that the horse is subject to a degree of 'wear and tear'.

They become more visible when the ground is hard and the horse is still being asked to compete and work hard.

Take them as a minor warning to keep an eye on how much work you expect of the horse if the ground gets hard.

Q. Using the horse in front of you, show me where the sesamoid bones are. What are their function and what possible problems can occur with them?

A. There are two sesamoid bones in each fetlock joint; they make up part of the fetlock joint in conjunction with the base of the cannon bone and the top of the long pastern bone.

They are smooth, rounded bones over which run some of the tendons on their way to the lower part of the limb and the foot.

The sesamoid bones are vulnerable to knocks from the opposite limb, especially if the horse does not move very well or straight.

The fetlock joint is potentially vulnerable to strain, which may result in inflammation of the sesamoid bones, which is then known as sesamoiditis.

Any bones or joints are susceptible to jarring from excessive work on hard ground.

Q. What are the main ligaments in the horse's lower leg? Show me where they are on this horse. Are there any problems that can affect them?

A. Be able to name and designate on the lower limb the following ligaments:

- Superior check ligament (just above the knee).
- Sub carpal check ligament (just below the knee).
- Suspensory ligament.

Ligaments can be damaged in much the same way as tendons, i.e. by pulls and strains (e.g. jumping into heavy ground or when the horse suddenly has to cope with a change of terrain or going).

Ligaments are less elastic and stronger than tendons but once damaged usually need a much longer period of recuperation to recover fully.

The horse's foot

Q. Assess the balance of the horse's front feet.

A. Be able to compare the size and shape of both front feet.

Be able to assess the limb alignment or 'column of support' down the limb.

Be able to consider the hoof–pastern axis and whether the weight is distributed evenly over the foot, from front to back and from side to side.

Q. What problems may be caused by the feet being incorrectly balanced?

A. The horse may not move fluently, he may pull shoes off.

He may wear his shoes unevenly and eventually he is likely to go lame.

There may be a negative effect on the joints further up the leg.

Q. Tell me about the hoof–pastern axis of this horse's front feet.

A. Make sure that you know what the hoof–pastern axis is and how it should appear (the pastern should slope at around 45–50° angle to the ground, and this slope should be in line with the angle of the wall of the hoof).

Be able to describe and recognise, on the horse if necessary, a broken-back hoof–pastern axis and a broken-forward axis.

Q. What problems can arise from an incorrect hoof–pastern axis?

A. A broken-back hoof–pastern axis puts undue strain on the back of the limbs, which might affect the tendons and ligaments in the lower leg.

A broken-forward axis may make the feet more upright and more vulnerable to jarring from concussion.

Q. Look at the wear on this horse's front/hind shoes. What can you tell me about this horse's way of going?

A. Unlevel wear on the shoes will tell you how the horse distributes weight on his feet (even if you cannot see him move).

Be on the look-out for the following:

- Worn toes (does the horse drag his toes?)
- Wear on the outside or inside of the foot or feet – this indicates where the horse takes more pressure on his foot.

Q. Do this horse's feet tell you anything about his general state of health?

A. If the feet are cracked or brittle this may reflect a poor diet.

If the feet show different coloured rings around the horn (not ridges) then this may indicate a period where there was a spurt of horn growth at a time when the horse perhaps had access to different or richer pasture.

Shoeing

Q. Discuss the shoes on the horse in front of you.

A. Be able to look at the front and hind shoes and describe exactly what you see.

Do the shoes look as if they have recently been put on?

Is the foot over-growing the shoe? Are the clenches rising? Are the shoes showing signs of wear?

Q. Where would you find stud holes?

A. Usually they will be visible as small round holes in the heel region of the shoe. They are usually on the outside branch of the shoe and more likely to be found in the hind shoes. Occasionally they may be in the front shoes as well.

Q. How do you clean out stud holes?

A. Pick out the hole with some kind of sharp instrument – a farrier's shoe nail will do the job.

Use a 'T tap' instrument to re-establish the screw threads of the stud hole.

Q. What can you use to plug stud holes?

A. To keep the hole from getting worn out or clogged up with dirt, pack the hole with some greased cotton wool.

Q. What type of studs would you use on hard ground?

A. Sharper, spiked studs will bite into hard ground and give security.

Q. What type of studs would you use on soft ground?

A. Chunky, squarer studs will hold more in heavier ground.

Circulatory system

Q. What does the heart do?

A. The heart acts as the pump for the blood in the body, pushing it around the whole body.

Q. What does the blood take to the various parts of the body?

A. Blood takes oxygen from the lungs to all parts of the body via the heart.

Blood carries water and nutrients from the gut to all parts of the body.

Blood carries hormones from the endocrine glands to other parts of the body.

Blood transports carbon dioxide and waste products from all parts of the body to the lungs and kidneys for disposal.

Q. How would you know if bleeding from a wound was venous or arterial?

A. Venous bleeding is usually less profuse; the blood will be red but not with the same intensity of arterial bleeding.

Arterial bleeding is likely to spurt from the wound (especially if the injury is close to the heart, where the influence of the heart's pumping is greater).

Venous bleeding (from a small or minor vein) will usually stop of its own accord. Arterial bleeding will definitely need veterinary assistance.

Q. How would the type of bleed affect your treatment?

A. If you suspect arterial bleeding you must seek help from a veterinarian and state the urgency of the situation.

Q. Horses' legs often fill when standing in. How is this linked to circulation?

A. When turned out, the horse is constantly on the move. As a browsing animal, it is in his nature to stay quietly on the move for much of his time.

When confined to the stable his natural movement is restricted.

Movement assists in the natural recirculation of blood and lymph up the limbs; the pressure of the foot coming to the ground assists in the blood being pushed back up the leg.

When stabled, this natural assistance is lacking and the blood and lymph tends to accumulate in the lower part of the limbs – hence the condition we know as 'filled legs'.

Q. After exercise a horse's pulse will be raised. What does the time it takes him to recover tell you?

A. The longer it takes for the horse's pulse to return to 'normal' the less fit the horse is and the more the exertion has affected him.

A fit horse will 'recover' much more quickly than an unfit horse.

Respiratory system

Q. Assessing the horse in front of you, what is his respiratory rate at the moment? Explain how you have come to this conclusion.

A. Watch either the rise and fall of his flank, or (if a cold day) watch the exhalation of his breath. A healthy horse will have a respiration rate of between 8 and 12 at rest if nothing is disturbing him.

Q. Identify some of the signs that would indicate respiratory distress and show me on the horse in front of you where you might see these signs.

A. Talk about whistling or roaring and be able to explain why horses suffer from these conditions. Know where the larynx (which these conditions affect) is located.

Whistling and roaring is heard when the horse breathes in.

Know about the Hobday procedure – a minor surgical operation, initiated by a Mr Hobday, to help treat horses with an obstruction to their breathing brought about by damage to the larynx.

Know about 'broken wind' (or emphysema) – a condition which ultimately causes the horse to be starved of air because the lung tissue has lost its elasticity. This reduces the lungs' capability to process oxygen and carbon dioxide efficiently.

Broken wind can sometime be accompanied by a 'heaves line' – a line along the horse's flank which becomes apparent when the horse tightens his muscles in an effort to 'push' out the extra air trapped in the lungs. This line is visible on exhalation.

Q. Show, on the horse in front of you, where the different parts of the respiratory system are located.

A. Be able to show where the nostrils, nasal passage, pharynx, larynx, windpipe, bronchi, bronchioles and alveoli would be in relation to the position of the lungs.

Q. Indicate on the horse in front of you how inhalation and exhalation takes place.

A. Air is breathed in through the nostrils.

It is warmed and filtered (by fine hairs or cilia) in the nasal passage.

It passes over the pharynx and larynx and down the windpipe.

The windpipe branches into two bronchi. (Each lung is supplied by one bronchus.)

The bronchus subdivides in each lung many times, to bronchioles, and ultimately into alveoli or sacs, which is where the exchange of gases takes place.

Oxygen is taken in and carbon dioxide is expelled each time the horse breathes in and out.

Q. What problems might be caused by an allergic reaction in the horse's respiratory tract, and what outward signs will be seen?

A. When a horse develops an allergic reaction to something, he becomes sensitive to it and ultimately may become extremely intolerant to it, his body reacting in an antagonistic way to the apparent foreign body.

He may show some unfamiliar and unexpected symptoms such as intermittent swellings over his body, filled legs or thickening of his glands around the jowl region.

Q. What problems may be caused to a horse's respiration by a full stomach?

A. The horse's stomach lies in close proximity to his lungs – the abdominal cavity (where the stomach is situated) being separated from the thorax (chest cavity where the lungs lie) by the diaphragm – and if the stomach is full and the horse has to work hard, the amount of room that his lungs have to expand is restricted. The efficient functioning of the diaphragm will also be restricted.

The horse may suffer digestive problems because the food cannot be digested properly because the lungs are making demands on oxygen.

Similarly the lungs may not get sufficient air for the work required if a full stomach restricts the space for expansion of the lung tissue.

Q. What aspects of either the environment of his stable or outside in the stable yard could cause this horse's respiratory rate to change?

A. Consider all the circumstances around you which might affect the horse: e.g. sources of sudden noises that might disturb him; horses coming and going, which could affect the quietness in the yard; vehicles which might start up and move about. His respiratory rate could also be affected by a dusty environment, or if he is too hot (wearing too much clothing) and/or if his stable is poorly ventilated.

Conformation

Q. Assessing the horse in front of you, do you consider him to be 'in proportion'?

Q. What problems in his conformation do you consider may affect his performance?

Q. How will his conformation affect his movement?

Q. When assessing the horse in front of you, what factors might affect his soundness for the work?

Q. In looking at the forelimb of this horse, do you consider the limb less than ideal or do you consider that the horse has a good forelimb? Please discuss.

Q. The horse's hocks are sometimes described as bow-legged, cow-hocked or sickle-hocked – please describe this horse's hocks.

Ailments/care of sick and lame horses

Q. Where on this horse would you find a girth gall? How would you treat it and how could you prevent it in the future?

A. It would be visible as a nick or bare patch of skin in the fold of skin around the area where the girth lies immediately behind the elbow.

If it is sore and the skin is red and angry then bathe first to soothe the region. If the skin is not broken then saline solution could help to harden the area.

Use a soft sheepskin type sleeve over the girth or work the horse without a saddle until the area is no longer red.

In future, use saline solution to harden the area prior to the horse coming back into work if he has been in soft condition with little work. Use a soft, clean girth and take care with the careful fitting of any type of girth or roller to prevent galling.

Q. What does ringworm look like and where on the horse does it usually occur? What action would you take?

A. Round areas of raised hair (prior to the hair falling out) or pink or grey patches about the size of a 50 pence piece.

Patches may be visible anywhere on the body, but are often found on the neck, shoulders, and face.

Immediately isolate the horse and monitor other horses that may have been in contact with the infected horse. Follow the isolation procedure strictly.

Consult the vet for the most appropriate treatment (usually an oral medication). It is often necessary to treat more than one horse in the yard to avoid a spread.

Take the vet's advice on washing the horse in an antifungal wash.

Q. If this horse had laminitis, what symptoms would he be presenting? How would you treat this problem and how could it be prevented in the future?

A. He would be extremely uncomfortable on his feet, attempting to alleviate the weight on his feet; he may draw his hind legs well under the body or tip onto the heels of his front feet.

The feet would feel hot and the horse would be very lame and reluctant to move.

Call the vet who would advise on the most up-to-date treatment according to what had been the cause for that horse.

Antihistamine injections may be used, as would some kind of pain relief.

If incorrect feeding has been the cause then this must be addressed for the future.

It is important not to allow animals to become overweight, especially in the spring, and ponies may need to have restricted access to any spring grass.

Q. You visit this horse in the morning and notice that he has a nasal discharge, runny eyes and looks listless. What action do you take?

A. Take his temperature (should be around 100.5 °F or 38 °C).

Offer him clean fresh water and some food to see how interested he is in eating.

Monitor him over the next few hours, but consider calling the vet if there is no improvement in him or if he has a temperature of more than one or two degrees above normal.

Keep him quiet and isolated from other horses. Make sure he is warm enough and has a good deep bed with a plentiful supply of fresh clean water. Monitor him constantly. Keep him comfortable, with his eyes and nose bathed to keep them clean.

Q. This horse has suspected colic. What are some of the signs of colic and how would you treat the horse?

A. The horse is restless and showing discomfort. He may paw the ground, kick at his stomach, look at his stomach, and get up and down in an effort to find a comfortable stance. He may at worst become violent, throwing himself around in pain.

Immediately call the vet. Colic can be very serious and the sooner it is treated, the better.

Remove the water bucket and any other moveable stable fittings. Bed down with extra bedding (if this can be done safely).

Monitor the horse constantly. If he is only mildly uncomfortable and it is a warm day, it can help to turn him out in a small paddock.

When the vet arrives, be able to tell him exactly what has happened to the horse in the previous 24 hours.

Treat the horse as per the vet's instructions and then give him good nursing care after his colic for 12 to 24 hours, or longer if he has been very ill.

Q. The horse had a fall while jumping. Upon investigation of his limbs you notice a swelling appearing on the back of one of his forelegs, between the knee and the fetlock. What do you suspect has occurred? How would you deal with this?

A. It is likely that the horse has damaged a tendon in the region between the knee and fetlock.

Immediate treatment would be to apply cold water (usually hosing the limb is easiest – for 15 to 20 minutes at a time, three or four times a day) or use ice packs if available.

It would be wise to consult the vet for professional advice on how bad the damage might be and what the best treatment is.

Tendon injuries always benefit from long periods of recuperation to allow the damage to repair itself, but the vet can advise on anti-inflammatory and pain-relieving drugs, which might help in the acute stage.

Q. What is a curb? Where on the horse would you find one? How does it occur and how should it be treated?

A. A curb is a strain to the ligament at the back of the hock, resulting in a thickening which is seen as a convex soft bulge on the back of the hock just below the point of the hock.

It occurs as a result of strain, sometimes with young horses working in soft and holding ground.

Some horses may be more prone to curbs if their hocks are rather weak or sickle shaped, which puts more strain onto the area where a curb would arise.

Usually they cause little or no concern other than a visual blemish. If there is any heat or pain while the curb is developing then it is wise to cold hose the area and rest the horse until any initial inflammation has gone.

Q. It is spring. The horse has been diagnosed as being infested with lice. Where on the horse do you normally find lice? How do you treat this problem?

A. Lice are usually found in the horse's mane and tail but may spread over the whole body if the infestation is allowed to proceed untreated.

Consult the vet for the appropriate treatment; he will advise on what is current and permissible.

Treatment will probably require two or three repetitions to ensure that the eggs are 'caught' as they hatch. Ten-day intervals between treatments are usually appropriate.

Q. What symptoms other than a cough lead you to diagnose broken wind or COPD? What could you do to alleviate the situation?

A. The horse struggles to work efficiently, showing signs of breathlessness and fatigue in spite of being fit enough for his work.

There may be a 'heave line' along the lower edge of his ribs, where he employs his abdominal muscles in a double exhale to try to push the stale air out of his lungs because the alveoli have lost elasticity and function.

Keep the horse as slim as possible and keep him fit.

Work him outside as much as possible and if possible keep him in an outside stable rather than an American barn type.

Feed him damp feed and haylage to avoid any dust allergies or implications from dry food.

Turn him out as much as possible.

Use dust-free bedding in his stable.

COPD is now known as Recurrent Airway Obstuction (RAO).

Summer Pasture-Associated Obstructive Pulmonary Disease (SPAOD) is associated with pollen and dust particles that a horse is exposed to especially in the summer months and has similar symptoms and treatment.

Q. Your horse has a fever. List the principles of sick nursing.

A. Isolate from other horses.

Warm stable with a deep bed and light warm clothing, bandages if necessary.

Ready supply of fresh water, with the chill taken off if necessary.

One person only to look after the horse to be able to monitor his well-being and to keep the risk of cross-infection to a minimum.

Small feeds of a succulent and palatable nature; reduce all hard feed and keep the horse on a laxative high-fibre ration.

Administer any medication prescribed by the vet, with a record kept of what was given, by whom, and when.

Peace and quiet for the horse but plenty of TLC.

Q. You are starting up a yard and need to stock an equine medicine cabinet. List some items you would include.

A. A safe, clearly marked lockable cabinet or cupboard that has the vet's telephone number and any relevant emergency numbers clearly listed on the door or inside.

A small variety of sterile dressings and bandages for emergency use.

Thermometer.

Small bowl (for treating wounds with saline solution).

Salt (if not in the feed room).

Blunt-ended scissors.

Gamgee tissue, cotton wool or similar material for swabs.

Some type of wound dressing (powder or cream).

Simple eye ointment (for runny eyes from flies).

Perhaps worm doses.

Perhaps a stethoscope.

Perhaps a twitch.

Q. Discuss some points that indicate good health/poor health in the horse.

A. *Good health:*

- Bright eyes, no discharge.
- Horse is alert, interested in surroundings, eating, drinking normally.
- Taking weight evenly on all four limbs.
- Horse looks at ease with himself.
- Coat glossy and flexible.
- Passing droppings and urine easily and regularly.

Poor health:

- A harsh, 'starey' coat.
- A horse that is thin and does not maintain weight in spite of appearing to eat well may be in poor health.
- A horse with a 'pot' belly may be suffering from a worm infestation.

Q. What is a poultice/tubbing/fomenting? What type of ailments would you use these treatments for? How would you apply them?

A. A poultice is used for drawing out heat or infection from a wounded area. It is made from a substance that holds the heat well (e.g. bran or kaolin) or can be a custom-made preparation such as Animalintex.

It can be used on any site where it can be attached, but is most effectively used on the feet or limbs.

Tubbing is used for the feet and can be carried out with hot or cold water, depending on the treatment. Hot tubbing would be to draw (similar to a poultice); cold tubbing would be to reduce heat and inflammation.

The heels should always be greased prior to tubbing to avoid any soreness arising from the heel region becoming water-logged.

Fomenting is a term used for applying heat or cold to an area. Sustained heat or cold is applied for a 15–20 minute period to promote circulation and blood flow, which in turn aids in the healing process.

Q. How do you take the temperature/pulse/respiration of a horse? What readings would you expect in a healthy horse?

A. Respiration is taken by counting the horse's inhalations and exhalations (breathing in and out); there should be around 8 to 12 breaths per minute in a healthy horse at rest.

Watch the horse's flank rising and falling; or in winter watch the horse's out-breaths, which will be visible in the cold.

The pulse rate is taken by feeling the horse's submaxillary artery where it crosses over the jaw bone (under the jowl). Feel the pulse with your index and second fingers. Count for 30 seconds and double it.

A healthy horse's pulse will be around 36–42 beats per minute at rest.

The temperature is taken by inserting a thermometer into the side of the horse's anus. Grease the thermometer and make sure someone holds the horse if he is likely to be anxious.

The thermometer should be read after one minute. In a healthy horse at rest it should be 37.8–38.3 °C or 100–101 °F.

Q. Discuss the four main types of wound that can afflict the horse. How would you treat them?

A. The four main categories of wound are:

Bruised or contused wounds – No outward break to the skin; internal rupture of blood vessels, causing discoloration or bruising, heat and pain on pressure; the horse may be in pain although the cause may not be immediately visible. Caused by a blow with a blunt object – commonest cause: a kick.

Clean cut/incised wounds – Easy to stitch, as such cuts have clean edges with minimal trauma; often minimal bleeding for the same reason; should heal easily as long as kept clean. Glass and metal cause incised wounds.

Torn or lacerated wounds – Characterised by tearing, with trauma, as cause is due to something rough, e.g. barbed wire; messy wounds, with edges not easily drawn together; often a lot of blood from torn blood vessels and much pain due to damage to nerve endings.

Puncture wounds – Characterised by deep penetration with only a small entry hole; easily infected due to healing on top with debris or infection still within the body.

Nails, thorns etc. typically cause puncture wounds.

Treatment of wounds in general requires skill, veterinary advice in any other than the simplest of cases and certainly if a joint, profuse bleeding or trauma is involved.

General rules for wound treatment would include stopping the bleeding, cleanliness, access to open air to aid healing, and attention to anti-tetanus protection.

Q. Your horse becomes cast in the stable. What does this mean, how does it occur and what action will be taken?

A. A horse gets cast in his stable when he has lain down in such a position that he has got stuck against a wall and is unable to gain sufficient purchase with his legs to enable him to stand up.

You may find him upside down on his back with his legs stuck against the wall.

You will need help and some sturdy rope.

One person reassures the horse at his head, in a kneeling position, keeping the horse's neck still and his head on the floor.

The second person wraps the rope loosely around the hind and front legs of the two legs furthest away from you (against the wall). The horse is then pulled gently over, using the ropes.

The timing is crucial. As the horse feels himself come free, he will struggle to get up. Both people should quickly move away from the horse on the same side.

Q. When would you isolate a horse? What procedures do you follow when isolating a horse?

A. You may isolate a horse when he first comes to a new yard to ensure that he does not transfer anything (e.g. a contagious condition) he may have brought with him.

Isolation would also be appropriate for a horse that develops a condition that you do not want to spread to the rest of the yard (e.g. ringworm).

Isolation procedure involves:

- Placing the horse in a stable away from any other horses (but still so that he can see something going on in the yard).

- One person only to look after the horse.

- Separate equipment (feed utensils, grooming kit, mucking-out tools, etc.) for the horse.

- A record kept of treatment.

- Bedding, uneaten feed, dressings, etc. burnt if possible to avoid infection.

- The stable should be disinfected after the horse has recovered and all bedding burnt.

- All rugs, tack, grooming kit, etc. disinfected, washed or cleaned thoroughly.

Horse Behaviour

The horse at grass

Q. What 'vices' make it dangerous to run a particular horse with a large group?

A. Biting or kicking or bullying.

Q. What characteristics make it dangerous to turn out a particular horse with a group of horses?

A. If a horse has strong male characteristics (in spite of being a gelding), he may 'herd' the other horses, especially if there are mares and geldings together, and he may fight with the geldings.

Q. What problems of behaviour can occur when mares are in season and running with geldings?

A. The geldings may become territorial and try to assert themselves as head of the herd.

Q. Do young horses and older horses run well together? How might the youngsters' behaviour annoy or upset the older horses?

A. It can work, but sometimes the youngsters will run around to amuse themselves and disturb the older horses, who are not interested in 'playing'.

It is important to assess each group and their behaviour and make changes if some horses are not settling and others are being disturbed.

The horse when stabled

Q. What stable vices would you watch for?

A. You could see weaving, crib biting, windsucking, box walking, tearing rugs, kicking, and banging the door.

Q. The new horse is standing in his stable swaying from side to side. (a) What is this called? (b) What would you do about it?

A. (a) Weaving.

(b) Try to make sure that the horse spends time out of his stable more than once a day; try to turn him out or exercise him on a horse walker if available; give him ad lib hay or something to 'play' with to occupy him; keep him in a part of the yard where he has plenty to look at to try to wean him from his habit.

Q. The new horse in the yard is described as being quiet in the stable and having no vices. What sort of behaviour would make you think he was wrongly described?

A. He appears agitated and unsettled, he may be pacing around the stable or banging the door.

He might exhibit a tendency to weave.

He is difficult to catch when you go into the stable; he does not come to you but turns his back to you and hides his face in the corner.

Q. What causes a horse to:
(a) weave?
(b) crib bite?
(c) windsuck?

A. In general, these vices can be picked up from seeing another horse behave this way; and there is some evidence that a horse can have a predisposition towards one or more of these vices from his gene pool.

A horse that is bored and confined to his stable for long periods is more likely to develop a vice than a happy, well-occupied one.

Q. The new horse is very nervous of people and is difficult to handle. How can you gain his confidence?

A. Put the horse next to a calm, confident horse who will give the anxious horse more security.

Appoint a competent, calm, positive person to look after the nervous horse to give him more confidence through the way he is handled.

Ensure a regular daily routine.

The horse when ridden

Q. Jogging is a bad habit. What can it be a sign of?

A. Anxiety on the part of the horse (or rider), bad training, or being 'fresh'.

Q. Your horse persistently refuses a jump he has been over before. What can he be trying to tell you?

A. The horse is telling you that although he has jumped the jump before, it was not a good experience for him and he has no intention of repeating it again:

- perhaps the jump had something to fear that he had not anticipated (a ditch on the landing side, water underneath, etc.), or

- the rider gave the horse a bad experience over the fence (jabbed him in the mouth, or sat heavily on his back), or

- he has repeatedly jumped this fence and is bored, or

- the tack may have hurt him in some way as he jumped.

Q. Bad management – overfeeding and underworking – may cause the horse to behave badly when ridden. In what way may this be shown?

A. If the horse is overfed and underworked, he is likely to be explosive and unreasonable to ride. He may buck, try to run away and generally be tense, sharp and unruly in his behaviour.

He may be so tense that he is bad-tempered with other horses, trying to bite or kick.

Q. What is meant when a horse is said to be 'nappy'? How does he behave and what are some of the possible causes?

A. A nappy horse will try not to leave his stable or his 'friends'; he will be reluctant to work independently and confidently on his own, taking any opportunity to try to take the rider home.

The horse may be nappy through inadequate training or riding – he has been allowed to 'do what he likes'. Leaving other horses has not been enforced and he thinks he can stay 'in the herd'.

He may be nappy through fear or lack of confidence in his rider.

Q. An older horse who normally jumps well begins to jump badly. What might he be trying to tell you?

A. He may have some pain or discomfort in part of his anatomy (teeth or back).

His tack may be causing him some discomfort.

His training may not be correct and he has lost confidence.

Q. What changes in behaviour might signify to you that the horse is uncomfortable, unwell or physically stressed?

A. Reluctance to go forward when he is normally easily forward.

Any change in the horse's 'normal' behaviour which is unaccountable.

Any change in the horse's eating habits or any underlying change in the appearance of the horse.

Any obvious sign of unlevelness in gait or non-acceptance of the tack being applied.

Q. A young horse starts rushing his fences. What is he trying to tell you?

A. The horse is indicating a lack of confidence in his training and starting to rush 'to get it over with as soon as possible'.

He might also be indicating an over-confidence in what he is learning.

Q. How can a nervous rider affect a horse's behaviour?

A. Horses are followers generally, not leaders; they need to take confidence from their rider, and if they are ridden by a nervous rider then a downward spiral can develop. The horse becomes less confident as the rider lacks the competence to develop the horse.

Care of the competition horse (as a groom)

Q. What health checks would you make to a competition horse on a regular basis?

A. General appearance; eating well; drinking; droppings/urine normal.

Temperature, pulse and respiration.

Thorough check of legs and feet when grooming daily.

Q. What checks concerning the horse's tack, shoeing, travelling arrangements and equipment, would you make prior to competitions?

A. If competing regularly then a consistent programme for checking everything would evolve. Until this is well established then a list would be helpful to avoid anything being overlooked.

Make sure shoeing is consistent and new shoes are not fitted in the last few days before a competition.

Make sure all tack is regularly maintained, checked and cleaned. All competition tack should be listed and checked into the lorry.

Make sure all requirements in the way of feed, water, forage and veterinary (first aid) necessities are listed and accounted for.

Make sure that the vehicle used for travelling is roadworthy, safe for the horse and has sufficient fuel.

Q. What preparations would you make on the day before the competition?

A. Ensure the lorry has fuel, oil and water; also check the tyres.

Make sure that all equipment was accounted for and loaded into the lorry.

Check the time of departure and make sure that the route to the competition is known and if necessary written down.

Make sure the lorry is clean, and a haynet tied ready for loading (if necessary).

Assemble all travel equipment the night before and have ready any grooming kit/plaiting equipment that will be needed in the morning.

Q. What actions do you take on the day of competition to keep stress to the horse to a minimum? Consider the various weather conditions that may prevail.

A. The more organised you are and the more 'normal' you keep the competition day, the more likely you are to minimise stress.

If everything is well prepared in advance then it should be easy to keep the day itself calm.

It may be necessary to have an earlier start than usual but, even so, the horse should be fed and his normal routine kept as near the same as possible, apart from the earlier start.

The more calm and relaxed you are, the less the horse is likely to get excited by the change of 'atmosphere'.

If the weather is inclement then you must use your judgement as to the clothing the horse will travel in. He should not travel in clothing that is too heavy or does not 'breathe'. Since he is likely to get hotter while travelling, and as long as the ventilation is good, he may be more comfortable in lighter 'wickable' type rugs for the journey.

Q. What checks and care would you carry out:

(a) On return from a competition?

A. Make sure the horse is cool and has travelled home well.

Check his legs for any signs of injury or fatigue.

Look at his overall well-being (is he tired? off his food? any other signs of abnormality?).

Have you made every provision for his comfort?

(b) On the day following a competition (consider stress, both mental and physical)?

A. Has he eaten and drunk overnight? Has he functioned normally (droppings/urine)?

Are his legs cold and clean?

Is he glad to greet you even though he may be tired?

He should be allowed an 'easy' day, either being led out for grass, or better still, turned out for an hour or two.

He should have his legs and feet thoroughly checked for any problems.

Always trot him up to check soundness.

(c) During the few days following a competition?

A. He should be checked for any signs of injury and lameness which may erupt a few days after the competition (e.g. a puncture wound in the foot).

Always monitor the work, the competition and the way in which the horse recovers after the competition. This will help to ensure that you are providing a well-balanced plan for the build-up to the competition, the day itself and the days after the exertion.

STAGE 3
The Exam

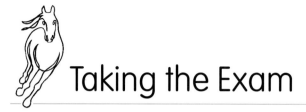# Taking the Exam

You should, by now, be developing a more confident approach to your exams and be familiar with the protocol of BHS examinations.

Exam psychology

- Remember to be confident and show the assessors your competence.

- Remind yourself throughout the day that you are well prepared and have both the knowledge and practical experience to satisfy the assessors that you are well up to the standard required.

- Continually remind yourself that nothing you will be asked to do or talk about will come as a surprise to you, because your Stage 3 knowledge and practice are sound.

- If something unexpected happens or a question is phrased in an unfamiliar way, deal with it as you would at home. If you are not sure what information is being sought, ask for clarification.

- React and deal with situations in a practical, confident way, leaving the assessor with the feeling that you would be capable of coping with minor crises if they arose in your work situation.

TIMETABLE/PROGRAMME
STAGE 3

PROGRAMME FOR CHIEF AND TWO ASSESSORS
10 Riding candidates
12 Care candidates

8.00 – 8.15	Candidates assemble	
8.15	Riding candidates walk jumping courses	
8.30	Candidates' introduction and briefing	
9.00	Group A	Riding on the flat
	Group B	Unit 1 – Practical stable management
10.00	Group B	Ride on the flat
	Group A	Unit 1 – Practical stable management
11.00	BREAK	
11.10	Group A	Ride over fences – show jump then cross-country
	Group B	Units 3a & 3b – Theory
12.10	Group B	Ride over fences – show jump then cross-country
	Group A	Units 3a & 3b – Theory
1.10	LUNCH	
2.00	Group A	Unit 4 – Lungeing
	Group B	Unit 2 – Practical oral
3.10	Group B	Unit 4 – Lungeing
	Group A	Unit 2 – Practical oral
4.20	EXAM ENDS	

BRITISH HORSE SOCIETY EXAMINATION SYSTEM

STAGE ONE

EQL LEVEL 1 CERTIFICATE IN BHS RIDING HORSES

Riding horses on the flat and over ground poles in the light seat

EQL LEVEL 1 CERTIFICATE IN BHS HORSE KNOWLEDGE AND CARE

Brushing off horses including putting on and taking off equipment
Horse husbandry, identification and handling
The principles of caring for horses

STAGE TWO

EQL LEVEL 2 DIPLOMA IN BHS RIDING HORSES

EQL Level 2 Certificate in Riding Horses on the Flat
Ride horses on the flat in an enclosed area
Ride horses over fences in an enclosed area

EQL LEVEL 2 DIPLOMA IN BHS HORSE KNOWLEDGE AND CARE

EQL Level 2 Certificate in Horse Care
Groom and plait horses and fit equipment
The principles of horse health and anatomy
The principles of shoeing, clipping and trimming horses
Fit, remove and maintain tack for exercise
Lunge a horse under supervision

EQL Level 2 Award in the Principles of Horse Care
The principles of stabling and grassland care for horses
The principles of watering, feeding and fittening horses

STAGE THREE

EQL LEVEL 3 DIPLOMA IN BHS RIDING HORSES

EQL Level 3 Certificate in Riding Horses on the Flat
Ride horses on the flat
Ride horses over fences

EQL LEVEL 3 DIPLOMA IN BHS HORSE KNOWLEDGE AND CARE

EQL Level 3 Certificate in Horse Care
Fit tack and equipment, and care for the competition horse
Horse health, anatomy and physiology
Lunge a fit horse for exercise

EQL Level 3 Award in the Principles of Horse Care
The principles of feeding and fittening horses
The principles of stabling and grassland care for horses

To achieve the BHSAI a candidate must be successful in L3 BHS Riding Horses, L3 BHS Horse Knowledge and Care, BHS Preliminary Teaching of Horse Riding and complete a portfolio.

STAGE FOUR

BHS STAGE 4 IN RIDING HORSES ON THE FLAT

BHS STAGE 4 IN RIDING HORSES OVER FENCES

BHS STAGE 4 IN LUNGEING

Intermediate Teaching, consisting of:
Teaching riding on the flat up to BD Elementary
Teaching riding over fences, show jumping or cross-country
Teaching an improving rider on the lunge
Class lesson, either flat or grid work
Deliver a presentation
Theory covering business knowledge and teaching

To achieve BHSII a candidate must be successful in both the Stage 4 and Intermediate Teaching Test

To achieve the BHSI the candidate must be successful in BHS Stable Manager, BHS Senior Coach and BHS Equitation

RIDING AND ROAD SAFETY

EQL LEVEL 2 AWARD IN BHS RIDING HORSES SAFELY ON THE PUBLIC HIGHWAY

The principles of riding horses on the highway
Ride a horse in a enclosed area and on the highway

COACHING

EQL LEVEL 3 CERTIFICATE IN BHS PRELIMINARY TEACHING OF HORSE RIDING

Coach a group of riders for improvement
Coach an inexperienced rider for improvement

EQL Level 2 Award in the Principles of Coaching Sport
Understanding the fundamentals of coaching sport
Understanding how to develop participants through coaching sport
Supporting participants' lifestyle through coaching sport
Understanding the principles of safe and equitable coaching practice

For information on UKCC Endorsed Coaching Awards and Certificates please contact the Exams Office directly for information.

What to wear

Turn out for the day must be neat, workmanlike and professional. As in any of the exams that you have already sat (BHS or Pony Club), you should wear beige, fawn or dark plain coloured breeches /jodphurs with clean leather boots, or short boots and leather half chaps, or a clean pair of rubber riding boots. A shirt and tie or stock with a tweed jacket completes the outfit.

Do wear gloves, and make sure your hair is neat and tidy (tied back or in a hairnet if long). Take an extra waistcoat or sweater if you want to take off your jacket during the stable management section.

Make sure you have a short and a long whip, and a body protector for the cross-country phase.

You will be given a sticky label on which to write your name. Use the name that you are familiar with being called, but make sure that the chief assessor has your name spelt correctly on the list.

Exam procedure

- The exam will take all day (see sample timetable above). Usually the riding and jumping take place in the morning, being run concurrently with some of the stable management sections.

- The stable management is split into three sections namely: practical, practical oral, and theory. You should be able to see from the text of the syllabus what is examined in each section.

- In the riding sections there will be a maximum of five candidates in each group; in the stable management there may be up to six in each group.

- Be polite to other members of your group(s) but avoid being influenced by them. Do not be drawn into conversations about particular horses used in the exam, whether ridden or used in the stable management tests. For example, avoid listening to observations which may go like this: 'The bay horse I rode is awful in canter; it won't go on the left lead and it stops if you have to show jump it.' Or: 'The grey horse in the third stable on the left has a splint on the near-fore, or actually I think it might be on the off-fore.' Information like this is wholly unhelpful and may affect your ability to assess the horse in a completely independent way.

- Make sure that you are focused throughout the day, demonstrating your competence in every section.

- Stay warm and dry, and take a packed lunch and plenty of water to drink. Drink water regularly through the day – it helps to keep you alert and concentrating.

- Make sure that you have some sturdy shoes or Wellingtons to wear when you walk the cross-country fences (and show jumps if on wet grass) so that you keep your riding boots clean for the ridden sections of the exam.

- Make sure that you wear gloves for the riding and lungeing and that you have your gloves and hat available for trotting up in hand and loading sections of the exam.

- Take a change of clothes with you so that if you get wet during the day you can change to drive home. You do not want to tackle a long journey home in wet clothing.

- At the end of the day give your arm number to the assessor who takes you for the last section, and make sure you collect all your belongings. You should receive your results by post in around five to ten days.

 Further Reading

The following books and booklets can all be obtained from the BHS Bookshop.

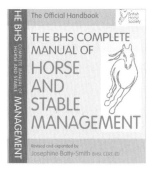

**The BHS Complete Manual
of Horse and Stable
Management**

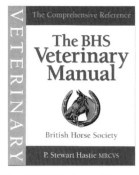

The BHS Veterinary Manual

**The BHS Complete
Manual of Equitation**

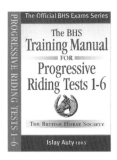

**The BHS Training
Manual for
Progressive Riding
Tests 1-6**

The BHS Manual for Coaching and Teaching Riding

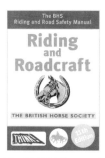

The BHS Riding and Road Safety Manual – Riding and Roadcraft

BHS Guide to Careers with Horses

Duty of Care

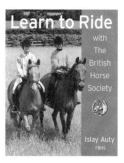

Learn to Ride with The British Horse Society

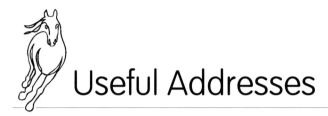# Useful Addresses

The British Horse Society
Stoneleigh Deer Park
Kenilworth
Warwickshire
CV8 2XZ
tel: 02476 840500
fax: 02476 840501
website: www.bhs.org.uk
email: enquiry@bhs.org.uk

BHS Standards Directorate

BHS Examinations Department
Stoneleigh Deer Park
Kenilworth
Warwickshire
CV8 2XZ
tel: 02476 840508
email: exams@bhs.org.uk

BHS Training Department
Stoneleigh Deer Park
Kenilworth
Warwickshire
CV8 2XZ
tel: 02476 840507
email: training@bhs.org.uk

BHS Riding Schools/Approvals Department
Stoneleigh Deer Park
Kenilworth
Warwickshire
CV8 2XZ
tel: 02476 840509
email: Riding.Schools@bhs.org.uk